# POGUE'S BASICS: MONEY

Also by David Pogue:

*Pogue's Basics: Tech*
*Pogue's Basics: Life*

.

*iPhone: The Missing Manual*
*Windows 10: The Missing Manual*
*macOS: The Missing Manual*
*Abby Carnelia's One and Only Magical Power*
*The World According to Twitter*

# POGUE'S BASICS: MONEY

Essential Tips and Shortcuts
(That No One Bothers to Tell You)
About Beating the System

--------------------------------

## DAVID POGUE

FLATIRON
BOOKS
NEW YORK

POGUE'S BASICS: MONEY. Copyright © 2016 by David Pogue. All rights reserved. Printed in the United States of America. For information, address Flatiron Books, 175 Fifth Avenue, New York, N.Y. 10010.

www.flatironbooks.com

The Library of Congress Cataloging-in-Publication Data is available upon request.

ISBN 978-1-250-08141-4 (trade paperback)
ISBN 978-1-250-08142-1 (ebook)

Our books may be purchased in bulk for promotional, educational, or business use. Please contact your local bookseller or the Macmillan Corporate and Premium Sales Department at (800) 221-7945, extension 5442, or by email at MacmillanSpecialMarkets@macmillan.com.

First Edition: November 2016

10 9 8 7 6 5 4 3 2 1

For the people who've
taught me the basics:
Nicki, Kell, Tia, Jeffrey,
Mom and Dad,
and Twitter

# Contents

------------------------

# Introduction

E very single person on earth would like more money.

If you think you're the exception—if you think you have too *much* money—it's easy to get rid of some. The rest of us will be happy to help you out there.

The question is: How do you get more money?

Well, you've probably heard the old saying "Time is money." And, yes, that's true. You can usually spend time to get money. By working, by learning a new skill, by looking for coins on the sidewalk.

But here's the problem with that "Time is money" thing: Time is *also* limited! You can't snap your fingers and have more of that, either.

So that's just great: We'd like more money, but to get it, we have to spend something *else* we don't have enough of?

You know what else is money, though? *Information.* If you know certain things, you can get more money without spending time.

As it turns out, the world is *filled* with little bits of information that can save you money or make you money. There's hardly a single area of life that doesn't harbor money-saving secrets. Cars, homes, hotels, planes, restaurants, clothing, hospitals, credit cards, insurance, taxes, movies… If you knew the ins and outs of every industry, you'd be a money genius.

You can probably see where all of this is going: to this book. Its purpose is to hand those secrets to you on a silver platter, so you don't have to scrounge for that precious information yourself. I guess you could say this book is designed to save you time *and* money.

## The birth of this book

I've spent most of my career writing about technology and science. Why am I suddenly writing a book about money?

The answer is simple: I have a character flaw. I cannot stand things that are inefficient, sluggish, or poorly designed. My brain spends its spare cycles silently finding loopholes, shortcuts, and better ways in every corner of life. I pick up "life hacks" the way another middle-aged man might memorize baseball stats.

When I see someone doing something the long way, I can't keep my mouth shut. I step forward, invading the privacy of total strangers, and demonstrate the better way. That's just the kind of helpful guy I am.

On one hand, this trait subjects me to the mockery of my wife and kids, who call me "Mr. Shortcut" (and not with the admiring tone you might expect). I often marvel that, for example, in 2016, we're still fastening our sneakers and running shoes using the ancient and clumsy *tying-shoelaces* method; my kids roll their eyes.

On the other hand, when I put together a book of *technology* shortcuts (the first *Pogue's Basics* book), I struck a chord. Apparently a *lot* of people feel overwhelmed by the featuritis of today's electronics.

I followed that with a second book, *Pogue's Basics: Life.* This time, I broadened my scope beyond technology—to everyday life. Traveling, cooking, clothing, shopping, driving, staying healthy.

And now, in your hands, you hold the inevitable Sequel to the Sequel.

I'm particularly proud of this baby. I've been a consumer advocate my entire life, constantly on the lookout for scams, overpricing, and psychological manipulations. I share my insights with anyone who'll listen. For me, the opportunity to lay them bare to a wider audience is pure gold.

I also asked my Twitter followers to share with me their own hard-won money-saving tips. You'll find some of their contributions in these pages, too, credited with their names italicized. (I also sent each contributor a signed copy of this book.)

## What's not in this book

Just to get your expectations aligned: There are plenty of money tips you won't find in these pages. Here, for example, are some of the categories this book does *not* contain:

- **The painfully obvious tips.** You know: Set aside some money for a rainy day. Cook at home instead of eating out. Quit smoking and drinking. Go to free days at museums.

Use the public library. Exercise regularly to save thousands in health costs over your lifetime.

That's all good stuff; they're just not really *tips*.

- **Time-for-money swaps.** We've sort of covered this already, but just to make it painfully clear: You won't find recipes for making your own toothpaste at home, growing your own crops, or ironing and reusing paper towels. All of those things do save you money, but at a terrible time expense.

- **Personal sacrifices.** It's also possible to save money by giving up comforts. You could buy a smaller house, drive a smaller car, eat smaller meals. You could bike 500 miles instead of buying a plane ticket. You could dry your clothes on a line. You could shift your sleep schedule so that you rise and set with the sun instead of paying for electricity to run lights.

  And if you're a guy, you could stop shaving. Pretty soon you'd look like Professor Dumbledore, but think of the savings in razors and shaving cream!

  (One tipster actually suggests that you peel apart two-ply toilet paper and use only one layer at a time, thereby making each roll last twice as long. Sorry, no.)

  If you're among those who have managed to make your life footprint smaller this way, I salute you! You're a person of tremendous self-discipline and enlightened thinking.

  But I'm after something more ambitious: making your financial impact smaller *without* shrinking your lifestyle.

- **Unethical tips.** The Internet teems with suggestions in the category that might best be titled "Abusing the System." You know: Help yourself to ketchup and mustard packets from cafeterias to save on store-bought condiments. Fill up on free dinner rolls at a restaurant, and then order only a cup of soup. Buy one movie ticket and then sneak into film after film all day. Tell your hotel that it's a birthday or anniversary so you get a free goody.

- **Investment tips.** Of course, the stock market is one of history's greatest money-making engines. But not only is investing a massive topic that professionals study for decades; it's also not surefire. Here, therefore, is this book's entire discussion of investment advice:

Buy low, sell high.

## What is in this book

What you *will* find in this book: ingenious, mostly non-obvious suggestions for saving and making money that rely on *information*. They let you know about quirks in the system. They don't require big time commitments, and they don't require you to make big changes to your lifestyle.

For example:

- **If you know the secret,** you can buy a $100 iTunes or Amazon gift card for $85. It's like free money.

- **If you're going to be away from home** for a couple of months, you can suspend your cable TV and Internet services. You can put them on "vacation hold," which means you won't pay for the service you're not using while you're away.

- **Service stations, oil-change shops,** and your father all may insist that you should change your car's oil every 3,000 miles. In fact, though, that's a myth that needs to die. Your car's manual (or Change Oil light) tells you the actual recommended oil-change frequency—which is between 7,500 and 15,000 miles.

So that's what's in the book: clever tricks that save you money—or make you money—on planes, hotels, groceries, taxes, clothing, cars, TV service, tires, Internet access, electronics, bathroom supplies, and much more.

## A few paragraphs about psychology

To really become great with money, you need more than a sense of economics. You also need an awareness of *psychology*—because, basically, money makes us crazy.

We pride ourselves on being rational, on being the animal most capable of reason—and yet we fall into psychological money traps every day. One study after another shows that our idea of the value of a dollar swings *wildly* depending on the circumstances. For example:

- **We're absurdly swayed by comparison.** Would you rather take a $50,000-a-year job at a company where your colleagues are paid half as much or a $100,000-a-year job where your colleagues make *twice* as much?

  If you were rational, you'd take the job that paid *you* the most: $100,000.

  But most people offered this choice say they'd prefer the $50,000 job—because they can't stand the idea of earning less than their peers.

  In other words, we tend to shop for things *relatively*, rather than assessing each offering's value independently. That effect is even more powerful when it comes to purchases whose value is hard to measure—like homes, paintings, or bottles of wine.

  Sellers take advantage of this all the time. If wine-store managers want to boost sales of their $18 bottles, they put $8 and $80 bottles on either side. Most people will instinctively reach for the $18 bottle; compared with $80, that seems like a terrific deal.

- **We're helpless at comprehending big numbers.** Our brains are trained to understand things through *perceiving* them. And we perceive small numbers all the time. How many people are coming to dinner? How many cupcakes will we need for the party? How many bedrooms does the house have?

Our *experience* is built on small numbers, so our ability to understand big ones is severely challenged. You can easily picture five soccer balls. But can you picture 500 of them? By the time you get to really huge numbers—a $19 trillion national debt, for example—all you can do is say, "Gee, that's a really big number."

Recognizing this blind spot in your own brain can help you make smarter decisions with your money.

- **Decision-making is exhausting.** Economist Daniel McFadden has written about many of the ways that commonsense laws of economics break down when the human brain gets involved. He points out, for example, that making choices is tiring. That's why grocery stores put candy in the checkout lanes: After a lot of decision-making in the aisles, your brain is fried at the finish line and doesn't put up much of a fuss.

- **"Free" blows our decision-making to smithereens.** Behavioral economist Dan Ariely once ran a fascinating experiment: He set up a stand in a store where shoppers could buy either a Lindt chocolate truffle for 26 cents or a Hershey's Kiss for a penny. The result: identical sales.

The next day, he dropped each price by a penny. The truffle was now 25 cents, and the Hershey's Kiss was *free*. Suddenly,

90 percent of shoppers chose the free Kiss, even though the *relative* price difference (25 cents) hadn't changed. We hear "free," and our normal judgment goes out the window.

- **Losing money affects us twice as much as gaining it.** Princeton professor Daniel Kahneman won the Nobel Prize in Economics for demonstrating some ways that money makes us irrational.

  For example, he identified *loss aversion,* in which we fear *losing* money twice as much as we like *getting* it. Most people wouldn't participate in a coin toss where they'd win or lose $1,000. Most people agree to play only if the prize for winning is at least *twice* as great as the penalty for losing ($2,000 if you win, $1,000 if you lose).

- **The base amount confuses us.** Happiness researcher Dan Gilbert poses a fascinating thought experiment: Suppose you could buy a car stereo at a dealer near your house for $200, but you could drive across town and get it for $100. Would you make the drive? Most people would.

  But what if you were buying a *car?* If a dealer near you offered it for $31,000, would you drive across town to get it for $30,900? Most people wouldn't bother. It's a 0.3 percent savings—who cares?

  Yet it's still a savings of $100 in each example. Why should our decision be different?

- **We're terrible planners.** We humans are *awful* at planning ahead. We wait until the night before the exam to study. We don't make small diet or exercise changes that will add years to our lives. We keep harvesting more fish than nature can replace, even though we know we're depleting the oceans for our descendants.

If we were purely rational creatures, we would make decisions *now* that would benefit us the most *later*. But we don't, and it affects our financial lives all the time. We keep buying regular lightbulbs, which need replacing every year, for $1 each—even though an $8 LED bulb will last 30 years. We sign up for cable TV plans because the first year of service is super cheap—and barely even look at what the price will be for the *rest of our lives*. We don't save for retirement.

If you were Mr. Spock from *Star Trek*, none of these effects would sway you. But you're not, and they probably do.

Now that you're aware of them, though, you can start noticing when they're at play—and maybe even resist them.

## All prices are made up

When Banana Republic has a "40% Off Everything" sale, do you think they're going to lose money on every garment they sell? No, of course not. The existence of that sale just proves that their usual markup is *more* than 40 percent.

When a cardboard bucket of popcorn at the movie theater costs $8.50, do you think it's some special kind of corn that's fertilized with gold and watered with unicorn tears? No; it's the same popcorn you could make at home for 90 cents.

The point, of course, is that in a capitalist system, every price, for every product and service, is arbitrary.

Yes, of course prices are affected by supply and demand, the convenience factor, market forces, regulations, and costs of doing business. But in the end, everyone who sells everything has to make up a price, usually with profit built in.

And in many situations, there's some wiggle room—and that's the secret behind many of the tips in this book.

## The ballpark savings

After each tip on these pages, you'll see an indication of how much money that technique is worth.

The author kindly requests that you spare him the class-action lawsuits; the "savings ballpark" is an extremely rough estimate, intended to help you gauge the general worthiness of a tip. It steers you not to an exact figure, but *maybe* to the correct power of 10. You'll know if a tip can save you, say, $30, $300, or $3,000.

Let's consider the tip called "Don't pay for cable while you're away" on page 104. The savings ballpark for that tip is $285 a year. Where does that number come from?

Well, the average U.S. household cable TV bill is $100 a month. Of course, bills vary widely, but that's the average.

You might go away for a month and save $100. Or you might be a "snowbird," spending the winter months in Florida, and save $600 a year.

So the savings ballpark for that tip is based on a savings of $300—right around the middle. Not the maximum possible savings—only a reasonable, typical figure. (Turning on the vacation hold itself costs $5 a month, so that's where the last $15 goes.)

In general, then, the savings ballpark figures give you an estimate of each tip's typical value. (The total value of all the tricks in this book comes to just over $61,000. Put another way, buying this book might be one of the best financial tips of all!)

# Chapter 1:
# Shopping Hacks

Here's the frustrating thing about money: As soon as you've earned some, the universe gangs up on you and demands that you *spend* it. Everywhere you turn, there's something else to pay for.

Fortunately, for every avenue there is to spend money, there's a loophole for spending *less* of it.

------------------------------------------------

## When to buy stuff

Prices fluctuate all the time. Supply, demand, the price of raw materials, the price of gas, location, the economy—it all affects product pricing.

You can't do much about any of that.

What you can do, though, is control *when* you shop. In certain industries, the prices for products always drop at certain times of year, like clockwork.

Actually, what's a little nonsensical is that there are usually *two* times for big price dips. First, there's the time when demand is highest (sales on toys before Christmas, TVs before the Super Bowl). Second, there's the time when demand is lowest (sales on candy after Halloween, bathing suits after swimming season).

Here's your master cheat sheet:

- **Bathing suits.** What store wants shelves full of swimwear that's no longer selling? Prices are lowest for the year in August, as the swimming season ends.

- **Bicycles.** New models roll out in September and October. That, therefore, is a great time to find sales on *last* year's bikes.

- **Cameras.** New models usually debut in February, so you can count on big discounts on *last* year's models on Presidents' Day weekend.

- **Camping gear.** Giant price cuts arrive in August; the summer's over, and so is demand for this stuff. Look for another rash of sales in October, too.

- **Candy.** Right after Halloween, every store and its brother slash prices to unload all the unsold candy.

- **Car parts and service.** April is National Car Care Month, so you may spot special sales that time of year.

- **Cars.** Many car companies roll out next year's car models in the fall, so you can get fantastic deals on the *current* year's cars around September.

- **Chocolate.** The fancy stuff goes on deep discount right after Valentine's Day (shocker).

- **Clothing.** In general, clothing for each season goes on sale a couple of months before the *next* season begins. In February, for example, they put winter clothing on sale for 50 to 70 percent off, to make room for the incoming warm-weather stuff.

Similarly, spring clothing goes on sale in May, to make room for summer items; summer clothing's price drops in August; and, of course, discounts on fall clothes emerge around November.

- **Computers** go on sale in September, once the back-to-school rush is over. There are more big discounts in November, on Black Friday and Cyber Monday.

- **Cookware.** As graduation/wedding season approaches, you can find good deals on kitchen stuff in April and May (especially Memorial Day weekend).

- **Cruises.** Sales on sailings usually arrive in January and February, when people are booking their spring break and summer cruises. In late October, there's another round of sales—both for people planning holiday cruises and for the cruise lines to unload cruise cabins that aren't selling well.

- **Electronics.** In late November, Black Friday and Cyber Monday have taken on mythic proportions in the gadget world. Every category of gadget goes on sale: TVs, laptops,

phones, tablets, cameras, and so on. Every store and online retailer fights for headlines, and the winner is you.

- **Fitness equipment.** January, after the holidays and while New Year's resolutions are still in force. *Huge* deals, from 30 to 70 percent off.

- **Furniture.** New models arrive every February and August, so the best deals (on outgoing models) are available in January and July. Also look for big sales in November, on Black Friday and Cyber Monday. Office furniture often goes on sale in May and October.

- **Grills.** The big rush to buy these is, of course, before July 4—so the prices drop right afterward. Prices crash again in October, as the weather gets cold.

- **Gym memberships.** The best deals, logically enough, sprout in June; that's when demand is lowest, as people head outdoors for physical activity.

- **Holiday decorations.** As you'd guess, prices crash right after each holiday. Buy Halloween decorations right after Halloween, Christmas decorations right after Christmas, and so on.

- **Home improvement.** Home Depot has its own special Spring Black Friday sale every April.

- **Jewelry.** Scout for deals in July, when there are no gift-giving holidays for miles to boost stores' sales.

- **Laptops.** Shop in June or during the back-to-school frenzy in August.

- **Lawn mowers.** They go on sale in August and September, when nobody needs them anymore because winter is coming.

- **Linens.** Look for the "white sales" in January.

- **Luggage.** New styles appear around March, in readiness for the summer travel season—so you can snap up great deals on last year's suitcases. In August, another round of price cuts settles in, since people are pretty much finished with their summer travels.

- **Mattresses.** The entire industry blows out last year's models over Memorial Day, so watch for crazy sales in May. More sales around the July 4 and Labor Day weekends.

- **Office furniture.** May.

- **School supplies.** August, of course. Back to school sales!

- **Ski stuff.** The big sales are usually in March, since nobody's buying gear for *that* winter anymore.

- **Sneakers.** You can find delicious deals as high as 50 percent off in April, as shoe stores try to shoe you up and shoo you outdoors.

- **Tools.** Shop in July, since Father's Day is now over.

- **Toys.** Are you kidding? January, right after the holidays. Everything's marked down. (Then again, you may also find some big sales *before* the holidays, especially on Black Friday and Cyber Monday.)

- **TVs.** February, to make room for the new models and to accommodate the Super Bowl frenzy.

- **Wedding dresses.** Nobody's buying wedding stuff in November and December, so that's when the bridal shops mark down their wares to make room for the new year's designs.

### Savings ballpark: $855 a year

*$855 = 5 percent savings on $17,100, the annual U.S. family spending on clothing, entertainment, and other consumer goods*

# Discounts on everything: RetailMeNot

If you don't visit RetailMeNot.com before you buy *anything*, you're crazy.

This site is a massive collection of coupons—both printable ones to use at physical stores and coupon *codes* to use when you buy things online. (Millions of fans find these deals and submit them to the site.)

You just search for the store you're shopping in or the thing you're about to buy. You'd be amazed at how many times out of 100 there's a discount waiting for you.

A huge collection of online and real-world shops, restaurants, and services offer coupons and discount codes here.

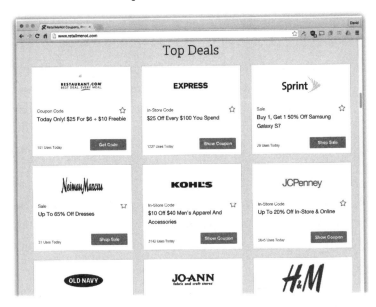

A few examples:

- **Babies.** Babies "R" Us, Diapers.com, Pampers.

- **Clothes.** Dressbarn, OshKosh B'gosh, Abercrombie & Fitch, Disney Store, Banana Republic, Ralph Lauren, Hanes, Under Armour, Forever 21, L.L.Bean, Garnet Hill, The Limited, Saks Fifth Avenue, Victoria's Secret, Old Navy, Aéropostale, American Eagle Outfitters, H&M, Gap, Lands' End, Sports Authority, Lane Bryant, Ashley Stewart.

- **Department stores.** Macy's, Amazon, Target, Sears, Bed Bath & Beyond, Kmart, Nordstrom, Lord & Taylor, Costco.

- **Drugstores/health.** CVS, Drugstore.com, GNC, Walgreens.

- **Electronics.** Best Buy, Apple Store, Verizon, HP, Newegg, Netflix, Audible.

- **Food (takeout).** GrubHub, Dunkin' Donuts, Seamless, Starbucks.

- **Gifts.** Edible Arrangements, FTD, 1-800-Flowers.com, ProFlowers, Teleflora.

- **Home.** Home Depot, Lowe's, Pottery Barn, Ace Hardware. (Also PetSmart and Petco.)

- **Office.** Staples, Office Depot, OfficeMax.

- **Restaurants.** Pizza Hut, Subway, Ruby Tuesday, Domino's, Olive Garden, Boston Market, Outback Steakhouse, Denny's, Burger King, Einstein Bros. Bagels, Chili's, Restaurant.com.

- **Shoes.** Payless, Foot Locker, Famous Footwear, Nike, UGG Australia, Shoes.com, Adidas, Converse.

- **Tickets.** Ticketmaster, Fandango.

- **Travel.** Airbnb, Hotels.com, Budget Car Rental, Avis, Enterprise, Hertz, SuperShuttle, Travelocity, Expedia, Priceline, Southwest, Frontier Airlines, Uber, Spirit Airlines, Hotwire, Dollar Rent a Car, CheapOair, Amtrak, Alamo Rent A Car, Park 'N Fly, Emirates airline, CheapTickets, Thrifty Car Rental.

The trick here is to *remember* to visit RetailMeNot whenever you're about to buy something.

There's an excellent free RetailMeNot app for your smartphone, too. When you're actually out in Shopping Land, about to make a purchase, you can check the app to see if this store has coupons available. The app can also make your phone chirp and vibrate when you're walking *by* a store with coupons available.

Bottom line: RetailMeNot is like free money. You should take it.

### Savings ballpark: $600 a year
*$600 = An average savings of 15 percent, assuming that you use RetailMeNot on half your purchases (average consumer expenditures on physical goods: $8,000 annually)*

---

# The eight great ways to get cheaper movie tickets

The movie industry got it all wrong. It predicted that if home VCRs and DVDs were allowed to proliferate, we'd all stop going *out* to see movies. The entire movie industry would collapse.

Instead, what happened? We go out to see movies more than ever before. Our habit of watching movies at home turned us into a nation of movie *nuts*.

Along the way, what was once the ultimate cheap family getaway has become an *expensive* family getaway. In big cities, movie tickets are $15 each, popcorn is $8, and soda is $5; add in parking, and suddenly you're looking at over a hundred bucks for the family.

Fortunately, if you're willing to plan ahead, it's possible to snag discounted entry to the multiplex. Let us count the ways:

- **Harness the power of the group.** You can read about Groupon.com on page 208—but one of its most attractive offerings is frequent deals on discounted Fandango tickets. (Fandango sells movie tickets to every theater near you.) A typical deal might be $16 for a pair of movie tickets, which saves you about 30 percent.

Fandango

$16 toward Two Movie Tickets from Fandango

Avoid the box office with convenient online redemption at more than 26,000 screens around the nation.

$26 $16

TRENDING          VIEW DEAL

AAA and AARP memberships get you movie-ticket discounts, too (pages 203 and 205).

- **Sam's Club, Costco.** These membership discount stores (page 212) sell discounted tickets to local movie theaters. You just have to ask for them at the customer service desk. You might, for example, snag a 10-ticket book for $85, which represents a discount of 15 to 25 percent, depending on the price of movies where you live. (Movie tickets are much more expensive in big cities than in rural areas.)

And remember: If you buy your discounted tickets using a cash-back credit card (page 46), the deal is even sweeter.

- **Discounted gift cards.** Gift-card exchange sites like GiftCardGranny.com and CardCash.com (page 58) are teeming with gift cards to the major theater chains, ready for you to buy for 15 percent off. If you're a frequent moviegoer, you really *must* buy movie cards there and start paying less.

| | Type | Quantity | Value | % Off ▾ | Price | |
|---|---|---|---|---|---|---|
| | Printable eCard | 1 | $7.00 | 15.5% | $5.92 | ADD TO CART |
| | Physical Card | 1 | $0.75 | 15.5% | $0.63 | ADD TO CART |
| | Printable eCard | 1 | $2.47 | 15.5% | $2.09 | ADD TO CART |
| | Printable eCard | 2 | $2.50 | 15.5% | $2.11 | ADD TO CART |

- **Matinees.** Movies that begin before dinnertime are often sold at "bargain matinee" prices—$6 or $8 instead of $10 or $12, for example. This offer varies; to find out, call the theater. Or pull up Fandango.com, click the movie showtime you're eyeing, and look at the matinee price.

- **The unlimited-movie plan.** At MoviePass.com, you can sign up for this most unusual program: For $30 a month, you can see *all the movies you want.*

There are no blackout dates, and almost all theaters are included. If you see three movies a month, you start coming out ahead. If you see more than one a week, you save a *lot* of money. Heck, you can see a movie every day—total price, $1 a ticket!

There's some fine print: IMAX and 3D movies aren't included. You have to pay the $30 a month for an entire year, or else pay early-cancellation fees ($20 to $75, depending on how soon you quit).

Otherwise, though, MoviePass.com is like Netflix for going out to the movies.

• **Join the club.** Every major theater chain offers its own loyalty program: Regal, AMC, Cinemark, Carmike, Showcase, Bow Tie, and so on. It's free to join. The more movies you attend, the more points you get, and you can redeem them for free popcorn, drinks, and movie tickets.

More to the point, you also get discount offers by email, a free movie ticket on your birthday, and other goodies.

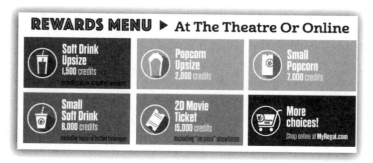

• **Be old or young.** Movie theaters offer student discounts and senior discounts—and their definitions of "student" and "senior" can be pretty lax. In some places, *over 50* is considered old enough for the discounted senior ticket.

- **See advance screenings.** Most movies host free advance screenings in big cities—for critics, for bloggers, for building word of mouth. Yes, we're talking about *free* movies *before* the public gets to go see them.

In the days of yore, the only way you'd get invited was to be on the mailing list of the PR company setting up the screenings. These days, though, you can register with Gofobo.com (or use its app). Gofobo lets you search for advance screenings near you—and you get invitations to them.

Two footnotes. First, they want to ensure a full house, so they distribute more passes than they have seats; you'll be told to arrive an hour early. (You'll also be told to leave your cell phone in the car, to ensure that you won't record the movie illegally.) Second, you may be alarmed at how much junk email you get once you've signed up. For best results, register with Gofobo using a *secondary* email address, so that your primary address doesn't get clogged up.

There are also, of course, free movie showings at schools, libraries, and town summer programs. And there are "second-run" theaters in most cities, where the movies are a few months old but also half-price.

### Savings ballpark: $115 a year
*$115 = 20 percent savings for a family of four, seeing one movie a month at $12 per ticket*

------------------------------------------------------------

# The truth about Gap, Banana Republic, and Old Navy

If you wander into one of these popular clothing stores and pay the price on the tag, you're a sucker. Plain and simple.

You should *never* pay full price at Gap, Banana Republic, or Old Navy. A single mother ship (Gap Inc.) runs all three chains, and they all follow the same fascinating business model: They price the clothes higher than you might expect—but then they *shower* the world with sales and discounts and deals. All the time. If you time your visits, you can walk away with great clothing at much lower prices.

Here are some of the techniques. (Most of them work identically for Gap and Banana Republic. Old Navy's savings mechanisms are similar, but the percentages may differ.)

- **40-percent-off-everything sales.** Gap, Banana Republic, and Old Navy run 40-percent-off sales every couple of months, often tied to holidays. The sales usually run for several days.

  The crazy part is that some items are already on sale when the 40-percent-off sale rolls around. That is, you can get 40 percent off the *sale* price.

  So how do you know when one of these sales is on? Visit the website (Gap.com, BananaRepublic.com, or OldNavy.com); you won't be able to miss the banner advertising the sale.

Or, if you're willing to surrender your email address, you can sign up for these stores' email newsletters, right there on their websites. They'll email you when the sales are on. As a bonus, the mere act of signing up for that newsletter usually gets you a coupon for 15 or 20 percent off.

- **20 percent off anything.** When you buy something at one of these three stores, along with your receipt, you generally get a little slip of paper inviting you to take an online survey. (Gap's survey, for example, is at survey4gap.com.)

```
         GAP - 0150
      890 MARKET STREET
    SAN FRANCISCO CA, 94102
    Tel. (415) 788-5909

3/9/17  2:38:42 PM
Trans.: 8301
Cashier: 1730293

20% off one regular priced item at Gap!
Complete our survey within 5 days from
    today and receive 20% off one
regular priced item. To take the
   survey, visit the web at:
        www.survey4Gap.com
At the end of the survey, you will be
given a discount code which you should
  record here: __ __ __ __
     Bring this receipt and
the code to a Gap store to redeem.
 Offer not valid at Gap Outlet or
gap.com. Offer applies to merchandise
   only excluding gift cards and
applicable taxes. Non-Gap products
are excluded. No price adjustment
on prior purchases. Cannot be combined
   with other offers or discounts.
Offer expires 3 months from today.
```

The survey takes about 15 minutes. When you finish, you'll be given a code to write on the receipt—worth 20 percent off anything on your *next* Gap or Banana visit. (Old Navy's code is worth 10 percent instead.)

- **10, 15, 40, or 50 percent off anything with the store credit card.** When you buy anything at Gap/Banana/Navy, the cashier will probably invite you to sign up for the store's credit card.

If you ever expect to shop at any of these stores again—or even if not—go right ahead. (You can use the same card for discounts at all three chains.) Card ownership works like discount magic:

First, you get 15 percent off whatever you're about to buy *right now*.

Second, you get 10 percent off anything you buy in the next two months.

Third, you get 10 percent off everything you buy on any Tuesday at Gap.

Fourth, you'll get frequent emails offering you discount offers exclusively for cardholders—usually 40 percent off everything. (In recent years, cardholders were invited to get *50 percent* off during the week leading up to Black Friday in November.)

Fifth, you get $5 back on every $100 you spend.

Finally, if you spend at least $800 a year, you get Silver status: free shipping on everything you order online, with no minimum order.

Note: This store-credit-card business is a fantastic idea *if you pay your whole credit card bill each month*. If you don't, you'll be slapped with very high interest rates and late fees. You've been warned.

- **50 percent off anything, anytime.** Work at the store. Employees get half off everything.

**Savings ballpark: $270 a year per person**
$270 = 30 percent off, shopping at Gap Inc. stores for half of the average American's $1,800 in apparel spending

----------------------------------------------------------------

# Meet coupons, 21st-century style

Back in the day, our moms clipped coupons from the newspaper. Depending on how serious they were about it, they wound up saving a lot of money over the years.

Eventually, many people quit clipping paper coupons. The time-money trade-off just wasn't good enough. Sure, you could save 50 cents on a bottle of window cleaner—but the time it took to pore through newspaper supplements, clip the coupon, keep it organized, and remember to use it was probably worth more than 50 cents.

But what if the Internet could *change* that time-money value proposition? What if that coupon-clipping session took only a minute and involved no actual clipping? You'd check it out, right? You wouldn't want to leave money on the table every time you went shopping, right?

The Internet is full of sites that round up thousands of coupons in one handy, searchable place. They include Coupons.com (the biggest one), RedPlum.com, and SmartSource.com. On these sites, you scroll through the hundreds of available coupons or just do a search for specific products. When you see one that looks good, one click (on a Print or Clip button) adds that coupon to your list of printouts-in-waiting.

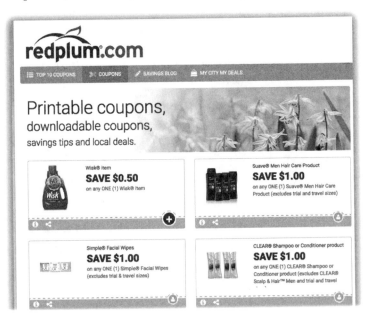

When you're finished browsing, you can print all the rounded-up coupons on a few printer pages, which you then take to the store.

**Savings ballpark: $312 a year**
*$312 = Three coupons a week, face value of $2 each*

-------------------------------------------------------------

# Tips from the cult of extreme couponing

It's possible to take the concept of couponing to an almost unhealthy extreme.

There are people, perhaps even some you know, who spend hours a week playing the coupon game. They seek out deals so extreme that the couponers actually *make* money by buying things. They have four subscriptions to each Sunday newspaper so they'll have four copies of the really useful coupons. They carry foot-thick binders full of carefully organized coupons to the store. They speak jargon like "BOGO" (buy one, get one free), "OYNO" (on your next order), and "Catalina" (the special printer at the checkout that spews out coupons *after* your sale is complete).

And they fill their pantries with $5,000 worth of supplies that, in the end, cost them only $300.

It's called extreme couponing. These people exist. They were even the subject of a TLC TV series, *Extreme Couponing*.

You, of course, would never take things that far. You plan to use the information in this book only to save money on things you intend to buy *anyway*, and you won't spend more than a couple of minutes doing it. Right?

Nonetheless, there's no shame in knowing some of the extreme couponers' tricks. They include these:

- **Stacking.** *Stacking* coupons is applying two coupons to the same item so that it winds up costing nearly nothing. Now, you're not allowed to use two manufacturer's coupons on the same item—two Crest toothpaste coupons, for example. But most stores permit you to use a store coupon *and* a manufacturer's coupon on the same item.

- **Competitor coupons.** Many stores accept coupons issued by *other* stores. For example, you might be able to use a Target coupon for some pain reliever at your ShopRite. (Not all stores will do this—you have to ask.)

- **Buy by the sale, not by your need.** You may not need deodorant right now. But hard-core couponers realize that, sooner or later, they'll *always* have to buy certain staples— paper towels, toilet paper, favorite cereal, ketchup, and of course what they call HBA (health and beauty aids like shaving cream, soap, dental floss, toothpaste, and shampoo).

  So when the deals come, take them, whether you're currently running low on those items or not. Buy five or six of something if the deal is good. Stuff them in your pantry or under-sink bathroom cabinet, and enjoy the rosy glow of knowing that you've planned ahead.

- - - - - - - - - - - - - - - - - - - - - - - - - - - - - - - - - - - - - - - - - - - - - - - - - - - - - -

# Local shops vs. the Internet

It's a classic dilemma. Should you buy something in a physical store, where you'll support a local business, boost the local economy, and get your purchase immediately?

Or should you buy it online, where you can save money?

Often, the decision boils down to how much lower the online price is. If that blender on the shelf in front of you costs $90 less online, then it might be worth ordering it instead of bringing it home with you.

That's the beauty of smartphone apps like RedLaser and ShopSavvy. You aim your phone's camera at the bar code on the package—and instantly, the app tells you how much that identical product would cost if you bought it from an online retailer.

Information is power—so, so much power.

## Savings ballpark: $300 a year
*$300 = 10 percent savings on $3,000 worth of consumer goods a year*

# Best Buy vs. the entire Internet

When it comes to electronics, the "Buy it online, or buy in the store?" debate isn't nearly so difficult.

Best Buy, the national electronics chain, has a price-match guarantee. It promises to match the price of any product at any rival store within 25 miles.

But who cares about *store* prices? What you really want is for them to match the prices of *online* stores, like Amazon.com or TigerDirect.com!

In fact they will. It's called the Best Buy Price Match Guarantee, and you've got it in writing—on the Best Buy website.

It works like this:

Find what you want to buy at a local Best Buy. Whip out your smartphone. Search for that item on all the usual discount online retailers: Amazon.com, Dell.com, HP.com, Newegg.com, TigerDirect.com, BHPhotoVideo.com (photo and video supplies), or Crutchfield.com (audio and video for cars, home theaters, and professionals).

Show the lower online price at the store's customer service desk. Boom: They give you the online price at the physical store without even blinking.

**Savings ballpark: $25 per purchase**
*$25 = 5 percent savings on a typical $500 appliance*

------------------------------------------------------------

# The shameful truth about extended warranties

For many years, *Consumer Reports* has been tracking product failure rates and extended-warranty programs. Want to know what they've discovered about extended warranties?

They're a rip-off.

Often, when you buy a new car, phone, microwave, camera, or whatever, you'll be asked—with tremendous salesperson encouragement—to pay extra for a longer warranty period. (Why the enthusiasm? Because the salesperson gets a commission on every extended warranty sold.)

An amazing number of us give in. For example, 40 percent of new-fridge buyers pony up for the extra warranty. They worry that if something *does* go wrong, they'll kick themselves for not having gotten the warranty when they had the chance.

The truth is, though, that an extended warranty is insurance. Or, rather, it's a bet—that your appliance will break *outside* the original warranty (say 90 days or a year) but *inside* the extended warranty period.

But the statistics show that they almost never do. If a new product fails, it's almost always soon after purchase, well within the original warranty period.

There are a few situations when the extra coverage is more likely to pay off: when you buy a used car, or a laptop, or a cell phone—as long as the policy covers *everything*, including loss and dropping.

Remember, though, that your *credit card* may offer extended-warranty coverage automatically. It's a common perk for credit cards.

In general, extended warranties are a waste of money.

### Savings ballpark: $160 a year

*$160 = Extended warranty prices for one major and one minor appliance*

---

# An Amazon Prime primer

No book about money would be complete without mentioning Amazon Prime. For better or worse, there's nothing quite like it in the world.

When the service began in 2005, Prime membership cost $80 a year. For that, you got free two-day shipping on anything. You broke even if you bought at least 25 things a year.

(Not *everything* is eligible for Prime delivery, but most things are. A Prime logo lets you know.)

Since that time, Amazon has raised the price to $100 a year (or $11 per month), but has quietly added a weird, random, but valuable list of perks to membership. Now Prime also gets you all of this:

- **Prime Video** is an unlimited streaming movies-and-TV-shows service, almost exactly like Netflix. They've got thousands of movies in the catalog, lots of entire seasons of TV shows, and a few original shows (produced by Amazon). None of it is quite as good or quite as copious as what Netflix offers, but it's getting closer. (You can subscribe to Prime Video alone—without all the other Prime benefits—for $9 a month. Of course, that makes no sense, since that's $108 a year—*more* than a full annual Prime membership.)

- **Prime Music** is like Spotify, in that you can listen to all the music you want at no extra charge. The catalog is far smaller, though—"only" 1 million songs are available at any time.

- **Unlimited photo storage.** You can set up your phone to auto–back up your pictures to Amazon Photos.

- **Kindle Lending Library.** If you own a Kindle (Amazon's ebook reader ), a Prime membership lets you read its 800,000

Kindle ebooks for free. They're often brand-name, worth-reading books. You can "check out" one free book a month.

- **20 percent off diapers.** Prime members have access to the Amazon Family club, which is basically a bunch of discounts, coupons, and sales on things you might need for raising kids. If you subscribe to one of the automatic diapers-by-mail plans, for example, you get 20 percent off. And if you make a list of goodies you'd like your friends to buy for you on Amazon's Baby Registry, and you wind up not getting everything on it, Amazon will let you buy the rest of the stuff for 15 percent off.

- **Early access to special deals and sales.** You can get at them 30 minutes before the rest of the world.

- **Free *same-day* shipping in big cities.** The fine print: You have to order before noon (seven days a week), live in a big U.S. city where same-day operates (27 and counting), and spend at least $35. (If your order total is smaller, you can pay $6 for the delivery.) And about a million Amazon items are available for same-day shipping—not everything they sell.

Some stuff, like groceries and essentials, arrives within two hours; everything else arrives by 9 p.m.

(The same shipping services are available if you're not a Prime customer; you just pay more.)

Overall, Prime is an excellent deal. If you place more than a few orders a year from Amazon and watch just a few of the free movies, you'll make your money back.

Prime is, however, what's known as velvet handcuffs: Studies show that Prime members tend to wind up buying *more* stuff from Amazon, and more often, than they otherwise would have.

### Savings ballpark: $732

*$732 = $20 saved on shipping two orders a month + $3 saved watching a movie a week + $8 saved on one Kindle book a month, minus $100 price of Prime membership*

-----------------------------------------------------

# Sharing your Prime account

There are two ways to spread out the value of your $100 Prime membership by sharing it with other people:

- **Share your Prime membership.** The cost of a Prime membership goes down easier when you realize that *two different people*, even in different places, can both enjoy its benefits. That includes free two-day shipping (even if it's to two different addresses), Prime Video streaming movies, Prime Music music, unlimited photo storage (two separate "lockers" for photos), Kindle Owners' Lending Library, and so on.

The one catch: To show how much you love and trust each other, you also have to share your credit card information with each other. (That's to prevent you from sharing your account with strangers across the Internet with the goal of abusing the system.)

- **Family Library** is a related feature. It lets you link two Amazon accounts, merging their collections of Kindle ebooks, audiobooks, and Kindle apps. You and your spouse, friend, or co-worker can share all your stuff with each other, for example, thereby not having to buy all those best-sellers twice.

You can also share your Kindle books and apps with up to four children.

Once again, the two consenting adults must be willing to share their credit card info to prove just how close they are.

### Savings ballpark: $300 a year

*$300 = $100 a year savings on a second Prime subscription plus $200 savings on books and apps that would have had to be purchased twice*

--------------------------------------------------------------

# More free months of Amazon Prime

OK, you're paying $100 a year for free two-day shipping. What happens if you order something from Amazon that *doesn't* arrive by the second day?

You just contact Amazon's customer service. (Visit Amazon.com/help; you'll find options to make this report by email, web, or phone.)

For breaking its promise, Amazon cheerfully gives you a free extra month of Prime membership or credits you $5 or $10.

### Savings ballpark: $8.33

*$8.33 = $100 annual Prime cost divided by 12*

# Eight obscure Amazon discount programs that shouldn't be obscure

Amazon.com, as you may have heard (over and over and over again), is the "everything store." You can find and order just about anything from this gigantic website, from clothes to medicine to farm implements.

Amazon realizes that it's at a disadvantage: It has no huge chain of physical stores for you to browse. You have to buy everything by mail order, sight unseen.

Yet Amazon dearly wants you to think of Amazon every time you need anything. So it's willing to give you *absurdly* low prices on things through about a dozen discount programs. Hardly anyone knows about them, but you should. Some are so favorable to you that you may wonder about Amazon's sanity.

- **Amazon Prime Store Card.** If you're a member of Amazon Prime (page 32), you should pay attention. Amazon offers its own "credit card," which works only for Amazon.com purchases. It gives you *5 percent off everything*, every time. If you shop on Amazon, it's like free money.

  (As usual, this amazing deal is useful only if you religiously pay off the entire bill every month. If you don't, you'll be slapped with a nosebleedy *26 percent* interest rate. You'll rue the day you signed up, and you'll use this book as kindling in your fireplace.)

- **Amazon Warehouse Deals** offers some incredible "open-box" specials. That's where somebody bought a product, opened it, and returned it without using it. Or maybe the corner of the product's cardboard box got dented in shipping, so Amazon can't really sell it as new.

You'll find Warehouse Deals offers in every category: computers, cameras, phones, TVs, video games, shoes, sporting goods, and on and on. Every single item has been inspected by hand and given a condition rating: New, Like New, Very Good, and so on.

(The quickest way to find Amazon Warehouse is to type *amazon warehouse* into Google.)

- **Amazon Subscribe & Save.** This plan is designed to give you two advantages. First, there's convenience: On a schedule that you choose, Amazon automatically sends you stuff that you consume all year long, like batteries, razor cartridges, baby food, toilet paper, makeup, cereal, shaving cream, pet food, laundry detergent, and so on. You don't have to remember, shop for, or carry anything.

Second, there are rather huge savings. Each thing you order comes with instant 10 to 25 percent savings. There's also a coupon section of the Subscribe & Save page, which takes even more off certain products. And shipping on everything is free.

But wait, there's more: If you schedule five or more items to arrive on the same day each month, Amazon gives you *another* 15 percent discount.

What you wind up with are some very low prices indeed.

(Easiest way to find this deal: Type *amazon subscribe & save* into Google. Or look for the Subscribe & Save logo on Amazon's pages for things you might need to reorder periodically.)

• **Student Discounts.** If you have an email address that ends in *.edu* (meaning a school, college, or university), Amazon will give you what amounts to a six-month Amazon Prime membership—for free. You get free two-day shipping, special offers and promotions, unlimited storage for digital photos, and free access to Prime Video (unlimited streaming of 40,000 movies and TV shows) and Prime Music (1 million songs).

After the free six months, you can become a regular Amazon Prime member for $50 a year—half price. You get that half-price deal for up to four years, as long as you're still a student.

You sign up for all this at Amazon.com/joinstudent.

• **Amazon Outlet.** You know what an outlet store is, right? It's a deep-discount store where retail stores dump stuff they can't sell: clearance items (out-of-season clothes), overstock (they ordered too much of something), and things with teeny imperfections (missing washing-instructions tag).

Amazon has its own outlet store, too, at Amazon.com/outlet. What you find here changes all the time, but it's usually clothing, electronics, and jewelry. Everything is brand-new, but the discounts are gigantic. Clothing, watches, and jewelry are usually priced from 50 to *80* percent off; electronics go from 20 to 70 percent off.

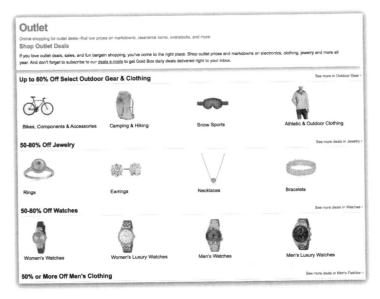

- **Coupons.** It might seem strange that Amazon has a page listing coupons that give you additional discounts on Amazon products, but it's true. At Amazon.com/coupons, you see a huge spread of coupons for familiar grocery-store brands: Planters, Heinz, Kleenex, Pop-Tarts, Keebler, Scott paper products, and so on. They're decent savings: 20 percent off or $2 off, for example.

You "clip" one by clicking the Clip Coupon button. Now you click the little photo of the product to see all of that brand's eligible products carried by Amazon: all the different varieties of Planters' nuts, or Heinz's condiments, and so on. When you click to buy, Amazon applies the discount automatically.

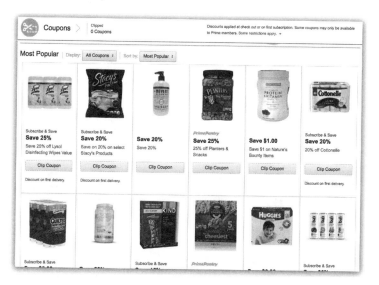

- **Gold Box (Deals of the Day).** Here's yet another page of Amazon specials. The rules are simple: crazy deep discounts (say 75 percent off)—and a totally random selection of things to buy. It's whatever Amazon wants to get rid of. A $37 Fisher-Price kiddie toy for $16. A $40 rotating iPad holder for $10.

    You can sign up on the Gold Box page (Amazon.com/goldbox) to get email listings of what's new, so you won't have to remember to check there every day.

- **AmazonSmile.** You can think of Smile as Amazon.com in a parallel universe, where half of 1 percent of everything you buy goes to a charity of your choice instead of into Amazon's coffers.

    All you have to do is start at Smile.Amazon.com instead of Amazon.com. From there, everything else works the same as it always has—but at the moment of purchase, you're offered the chance to choose *which* charity you want to benefit. (At least a million charities participate, so you shouldn't have trouble finding a worthy cause.)

Of course, AmazonSmile doesn't save you any money on your purchase. But it helps to improve the world without costing you a penny.

## Savings ballpark: $480 a year

*$480 = 5 percent off the average Prime member's $1,500 worth of Amazon expenditures with the Prime Store Card + 20 percent off $500 worth of Amazon Warehouse goods + 5 percent savings on $500 worth of Subscribe & Save items + 35 percent savings on $500 worth of Amazon Outlet purchases + 15 percent savings on $200 worth of couponed goods + 75 percent off one $100 Gold Box purchase*

# Price checks that go back in time with CamelCamelCamel.com

It might seem weird that a website exists to do *nothing* but track prices of things sold by Amazon.com.

But that's exactly the purpose of CamelCamelCamel.com (and, yes, that's really its name).

Amazon employs dynamic pricing, meaning that its prices constantly fluctuate based on all kinds of factors (time of year, popular demand, competitors' prices, and so on). Obviously, you want to do your buying when the prices of things are lowest, right?

CamelCamelCamel is how you find out. It has two key features:

- **It lets you know when a price drops.** There's a search box. You type into it whatever kind of product you're eyeing, either generally (*memory card*) or specifically (*sandisk ultra 32gb*).

  Click the one that looks good, and then type in a price where you'd bite. If the price ever drops to that level, CamelCamelCamel will email you to let you know.

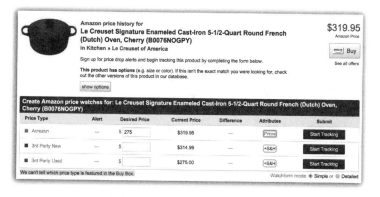

- **It shows the price history for any item.** CamelCamelCamel tracks the price fluctuations of 18 million products sold on Amazon. The idea here is that if you're about to buy something, you can see if you're buying it at a good time. You don't want to buy that toaster oven during a price spike, for example.

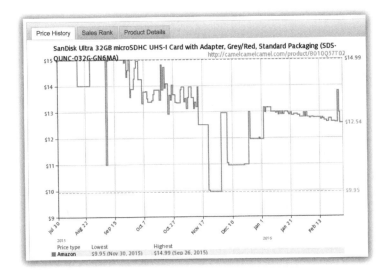

So how does all of this save you money? For years, Amazon offered a price-protection guarantee. If the price for something you'd bought dropped within a week after delivery, you were entitled to a refund for the difference.

Sadly, the growing popularity of CamelCamelCamel and other price-trackers eventually began to annoy Amazon. In summer 2016, as a result, Amazon ended its price-match guarantee program (except on TV sets).

But CamelCamelCamel can still save you money. It lets you wait to pounce until the site lets you know about a price drop.

If you're patient, therefore, you gain both savings—and a deep, deep feeling of satisfaction from having beaten the system.

## Savings ballpark: $70 a year

*$70 = 10 percent savings on the average consumer's $3,500 worth of purchases on consumer goods, assuming that CamelCamelCamel succeeds in finding deals 20 percent of the time*

# Chapter 2:
# Credit Cards

You know how banks make money from credit cards, don't you? All month long, you use your card to buy things without actually giving up any money of your own. The *bank* pays the stores, restaurants, and businesses. Your money sits safely in your checking or savings account.

That system is a wonderful gift, but it's not because the bank loves you. At the end of the month, you're supposed to pay the bank back for everything you spent that month.

If you do, great! You got the use of that bank's money for free. If you have the right credit card (read on), you even got *paid* a few percent as a cheerful bonus.

The banks, of course, hope that you *won't* pay them back promptly. If you don't pay off the full amount at the end of the month, they get to charge you an *insane* amount for the loan they've essentially made you—around 15 percent a year. (That's known as the APR—the annual percentage rate.)

And if you don't prove that you're making an effort to repay what you owe, by paying a minimum amount the bank specifies, you get into serious loan-shark territory. The penalty rates hover around *28 percent.*

No wonder the banks offer cash back and rewards for using their credit cards. The more people they can persuade to "charge it," the greater the number of people who *won't* pay off their bills completely.

That strategy works fantastically well—for the banks. At this moment, *40 percent* of Americans don't pay off the bill in full each month. The average American owes $9,600 to credit card companies.

If you're interested in getting through life with the most money, then the lesson is obvious: Do everything in your power not to carry a balance (that is, not to owe the bank). Pull out every stop—psychological, financial, practical—to avoid this massive money drain.

Every one of the "use your credit card to beat the system" tips in this book, therefore, should bear a footnote in bold italics: *This trick assumes that you'll pay off your entire bill every month.*

------------------------------------------------------------

# Use a credit card that pays you back

If you're smart, you'll get yourself a credit card that gives you cash back. The best ones credit you with, for example, 2 percent of everything you buy—and 5 percent on certain kinds of spending, like restaurants or travel.

The particulars of these deals change all the time, and there's fine print everywhere. But here are a few examples:

- **Citi Double Cash card.** No annual fee. 2 percent back on everything—no limits.

- **Fidelity Rewards Visa Signature card.** No annual fee. 2 percent back on everything—no limits. The one footnote: Your cash back gets deposited into a Fidelity account of some kind (a brokerage account, retirement account, cash management account, and so on). From there, you can withdraw it whenever you'd like.

- **Chase Freedom card.** No annual fee. You get 1 percent back on everything you spend, and *5 percent* back on spending in certain categories (on your first $1,500 in spending each month). Which categories? It rotates through the year: groceries, gas stations, Amazon, and so on. They also give you $150 as a thank-you for signing up.

- **Blue Cash Everyday card (American Express).** No annual fee. You get 1 percent back on everything; 2 percent back on gas; and 3 percent back on groceries (on your first $6,000 of grocery spending annually). You also get $100 as a sign-up bonus.

- **Blue Cash Preferred card (American Express).** This one has a $75 annual fee. But for that you get 1 percent back on most purchases, 3 percent back on gas, and *6 percent* back on groceries (on your first $6,000 of grocery spending each year). If you're the kind of person who eats food, you'll earn back the $75 fee

pretty quickly. Besides, there's a $150 sign-up bonus.

If you're not using a cash-back card, you're making a big mistake. It's free money. It's 2 percent off everything you ever buy—with zero effort on your part.

### Savings ballpark: $633 a year

$633 = 2 percent cash back on the average American's annual rewards-card spending of $10,680 + 3 percent back on the average American's $2,000 annual gas spending + 6 percent back on $6,000 worth of groceries

--------------------------------------------------------

# The argument for paying for insurance with a credit card

All major insurance companies let you pay for your insurance with a credit or debit card (Progressive, GEICO, State Farm, Allstate, Esurance, and so on).

And you know what? You should. Because if you have a rewards or cash-back credit card (as the previous tip strenuously advises), you're getting rewards or cash back on a *big* expense: the thousands a year you spend on insurance. If you have a typical $900-a-year car insurance plan, your card will kick back $18 each year; if you spend $3,000 a year on homeowners insurance, your card will refund $60 every year.

You've got several kinds of insurance to pay. You've got utility bills, too—same trick. It adds up handsomely.

As a handy bonus, you can set up a recurring automatic charge to your card each month. That way you never forget to pay your premium (and never have to bother).

### Savings ballpark: $120 a year

$120 = 2 percent back on the average annual car insurance premium of $907 per car + homeowners insurance of $1,750 + household utilities of $3,360

# The argument for paying your taxes with a credit card

The IRS doesn't accept credit card payments. That's too bad, really; your tax payments are generally some of the largest expenditures you'll make all year. And if you have a credit card that gives you cash back, frequent-flier points, or some other reward, you could *really* enjoy April 16.

Fortunately, the IRS says it's OK for *other* companies to pay your taxes on your behalf—companies that do accept credit cards. You can pay your federal taxes through, for example, Pay1040.com or PayUSATax.com. (Your ability to pay *state* taxes this way varies by state.)

You knew there'd be a catch, didn't you? And there is: These services charge a fee. It's 1.87 percent for Pay1040.com and 1.99 percent for PayUSATax.com.

Suppose you made $150,000 in taxable income this year, and you're filing your taxes as the head of your household. You'll owe $32,434.50 in federal taxes.

The best cash-back cards (page 46) give you 2 percent back on all your spending. So if you pay your federal tax with such a card (and your credit limit is high enough to cover that payment), you'll get $649 cash back. Of course, you'll have spent $607 in Pay1040 fees, so your profit will be $42.

But it gets better: The Pay1040 fee is tax-deductible! That fee lowers your taxable income by $607, which saves you another $170 on your taxes. When the dust settles, by paying your taxes with your cash-back card, you'll have saved $212.

Saving money is only part of the point here, though. There may be other good reasons to pay taxes by credit card. Sometimes you want to rack up expenditures in order to get a sign-up bonus from a certain card, or a spending-threshold bonus. Maybe you have a card that gives you frequent-flier points or hotel points for every dollar spent; paying your taxes this way would be a very quick way to earn a couple of free flights.

Note: Do not use your credit card to *finance* your tax payments; you'll wind up getting hosed in fees and interest. (If you need to pay your taxes on an installment plan, the government's own financing programs are much more reasonable.) Use these techniques only if you can pay off the card in full at the end of the month.

### Savings ballpark: $212 a year, plus free flights

*$212 = 2 percent cash back on the federal taxes on a $150,000 annual income, minus the Pay1040 fee of 1.87 percent + the tax savings from deducting the Pay1040 fee*

# The two smartest ways to kill your credit card debt

If you're among the millions who owe money on their credit cards, the first financial step in your life should be this: *Pay off the darned card.*

Of course, that's usually impossible at the moment; if you had the money available, you'd have paid it already. So the second financial step is this: *Pay less for that debt.*

Use one of these strategies:

- **Take out a loan.** Visit a bank, or do some comparisons online, to explore taking out an unsecured personal loan (also called a "signature loan") or a home-equity loan. The interest rate might be in the range of 6 to 10 percent, depending on your credit score. Since your credit card interest rate is much higher, it makes sense to use the loan money to pay off your card debt.

  Boom: You've just replaced a 28 percent interest rate with a 10 percent rate (for example). And you've got yourself only a single, fixed monthly payment to make.

  To make this tactic work, you should then *stop* racking up new debt on your card. Otherwise, you'll defeat the whole purpose.

- **Pay off the card with a balance-transfer card.** It might sound deranged to pay off one credit card with *another* credit card, but that's exactly the idea here. The trick: You get a *new* card that offers a starter period, maybe 15 or 18 months, when the interest rate is *zero*. You'll have that time to pay off what you owe on the first card—without racking up interest charges that make the debt even bigger.

This trick isn't some big sneaky shenanigan; the banks actually *encourage* it. At this writing, for example, the Chase Slate card (no annual fee) gives you 15 months of zero interest rate—and, unlike most balance-transfer cards, it doesn't charge you a "transfer fee" to switch over your debt.

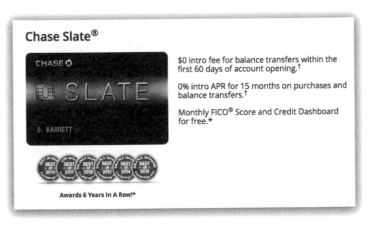

Another example: the BankAmericard gives you *18* months with zero interest. There's a balance-transfer fee of 3 percent, but that's still much better than the 15 percent you're probably paying now.

Use the balance-transfer trick only if you're confident that you *can* pay off the debt within the starter period. Because if not, at the end of that period, you'll be slapped with an even *higher* interest rate than what you've got now.

### Savings ballpark: $2,826 a year
*$2,826 = 18 percent annual interest saved with a bank loan (vs. credit card interest) on $15,700 (the average credit card balance among Americans who owe on their cards)*

# Debt-consolidation services: the angels and the devils

If you're stuck with a bunch of credit card debts, you may hear, on the radio or in the locker room, about debt consolidation services. They promise to roll up all your debts into a single, more manageable monthly payment. They negotiate *lower* interest rates from the people you owe, giving you the chance to dig your way out.

In fact, though, there are two categories of debt-help services—and one of them is extremely risky.

- **For-profit debt-relief companies.** These companies (the ones you've probably heard advertised) say they'll negotiate with the people you owe, resulting in a single, lower monthly payment that lets you dig out of debt.

  Three problems, though. First, these firms charge for their services; they become another group you owe. Second, they often advise you *to stop paying any bills* until they've finished their negotiations, but that suggestion means that you'll rack up huge penalties and interest while the process is going on. You may wind up deeper in debt than when you started.

  Finally, that "stop paying your bills" business can do real damage to your credit score (page 256).

  According to the CFPB (the Consumer Finance Protection Bureau—your government at work), you should avoid these for-profit debt-relief companies at all costs. Especially ones that (a) charge you up-front, (b) mention "a new government program" to bail out credit card debt, or (c) guarantee that they can make your debt go away.

- **Nonprofit credit counseling services.** Nonprofit services are a different story. You meet with a trained debt expert who studies your situation, gives you advice, and comes up with a debt-management plan. Instead of dealing with a mess of bills and creditors, you'll write only one steady check each month: to the counseling agency. The counselor does the work of paying the people you owe.

The debt plan is usually calculated to eliminate your debt within three to five years. Overall, you'll pay less each month, because the counselors work directly with your creditors. You can expect to get penalty fees forgiven, interest rates lowered (or even eliminated), and repayment deadlines relaxed. The creditors also agree to quit harassing you with late fees and collection-company calls.

For your part, you're generally required to *cancel* your credit cards. That may be a tough pill to swallow, but it forces you to avoid making the problem worse.

The counseling outfit may take a small fee out of your monthly payments for its services, but it's nothing like the gouging you'll get from the commercial companies.

To find a good counseling service, you can start at the websites of the National Foundation for Credit Counseling (NFCC.org) or the Financial Counseling Association of America (FCAA.org).

-------------------------------------------------------------

# The easiest way to get a lower interest rate: Ask for it

As you read about credit counseling services, a voice deep in your brain might be saying: "Wait a minute. These counselors negotiate lower interest rates on my credit cards? How do they do that?"

Easy: They *ask* for it.

And here's the crazy thing: You can do that, too.

In the end, these companies don't *want* you to go bankrupt; they would much rather get paid. That's why they're usually willing to work with you—to lower your interest rate, lower the minimum monthly payment, or waive some fees. You just have to ask. People do it all the time.

Before you call, figure out exactly what you'll be able to pay and when. You'll tell the agent, "My statement says the minimum payment is $215. I can't do that right now, but I could definitely pay $45 a month for the next four months. I expect to have a job by September" (or whatever the case may be).

Call the customer service number. Ask for someone who can change your interest rate. Once you've got that person on the phone, explain how much you think you'll be able to pay during your own personal economic downturn. Let them know you'll follow up by sending some documentation, like the budget you've worked up. Be calm and polite; you're asking for a favor here.

All of this works best if you contact the credit card company *early* in your crunch, when you're still *anticipating* the tough times. It works best if you have a good credit score, a good history of paying on time, and a plan for getting back on your feet.

Everybody has temporary setbacks. Maybe you're between jobs or your kid got sick. As long as the bank thinks it's just helping you through a slump, you'll get good results.

---

# The Target REDcard

If you shop at Target, you should apply for this card. It's available as a debit card or a credit card.

It gives you 5 percent off everything you buy at Target, free shipping from Target.com, and 30 extra days to return something.

All for free.

Now *that's* right on target. —*Abdulla Al Dabbagh*

### Savings ballpark: $120 a year
$120 = 5 percent back on $200 a month spent at Target

# Chapter 3:
# Gift-Card Hacks

OK, we need to talk about gift cards.

What a racket, man. It's a cash cow so big you can hear it mooing from the moon.

You buy a gift card for your uncle's birthday—let's say a $50 card to use at Target. Right off the bat, he could misplace it or file it away and *never use it*. That, in fact, is exactly what happens to about 20 percent of all gift cards, according to *Consumer Reports*. Your $50 now belongs to Target. For the store, it's 100 percent profit.

OK, what about when your uncle *does* buy something with your card? Well, Target comes out ahead then, too. He'll have a hard time spending *exactly* $50. So either his purchase comes in *under* $50, in which case Target gets to keep the *rest* of that $50 for free—or he buys something that costs *more,* in which case Target does a happy dance.

As the gift giver, of course, what your uncle does isn't your concern. You've done your duty. You've given him a birthday gift, and you're off the hook. (There's no shame in it, either; a majority of Americans say they *like* getting gift cards.)

But what probably hasn't occurred to you is how you can *profit* from the gift-card racket. You can make money on them *and* save money on them. You just have to start viewing gift cards as something more than a lazy person's last-minute gift idea.

---

# How to get cash for a gift card you'll never use

What if *you've* been given a gift card? Maybe one that you doubt you'll spend because it's a store you don't use?

This is why you should know about CardCash.com. It's a website that buys people's gift cards. With cash. Not full value, of course, but more than zero (which is what they would be worth sitting in a drawer). Depending on how popular your card type is, you might get 65 or 90 percent of its value in cash.

So if you've been given one and you're pretty sure you'll never use it, by all means: Sell it.

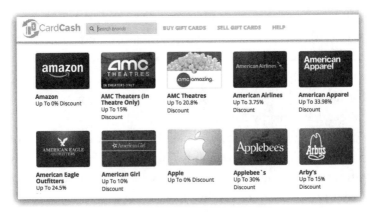

(CardCash.com is the largest such card-exchange site, but there are many others, including Raise.com, CardPool.com, GiftCardGranny.com, and GiftCardRescue.com.)

**Earnings ballpark: $150 a year**
*$150 = Two $100 gift cards, sold for $75 each*

------------------------------------------------

# Buy gift cards for yourself, pay less for things

You just learned about CardCash.com and CardPool.com. Now take it a step further: If you spot a card there for a store you use, buy the card for *yourself* and simply enjoy the savings. Take your pick. Barnes & Noble, CVS, Gap, Lowe's, Target, Banana Republic, Best Buy, Bed Bath & Beyond, GameStop, Home Depot, Macy's, and on and on.

The gift cards sell for less than their face value. So you can buy a $100 iTunes gift card for $85, for example, or a $40 Starbucks card for $32. If you're in the market for a gift card, it's like free money.

**Savings ballpark: $150 a year**
*$150 = 15 percent discount on $1,000 worth of cards*

------------------------------------------------

# These 14 states make gift cards even more useful

Don't you hate it when someone gives you a gift card but it expires before you've had a chance to use it?

Fortunately, Congress has your back. Thanks to a 2009 bill called the Credit Card Accountability Responsibility and Disclosure Act (the "CARD Act," get it?), you have certain protections. One is that cards can't expire for five years.

Many states have passed even juicier laws—like California's, which says that if there's a small amount left on the card, the store has to give you cash for it.

Just so you have it, here are the 14 states that have done the federal law one better (or several better):

- **California.** California has the strongest gift-card laws in the country. Gift cards are never allowed to expire. And if there's less than $10 left on a card, the store *has* to give you cash for that remaining value.

- **Colorado.** If there's less than $5 of value on the card, the store has to give it to you in cash.

- **Connecticut.** Gift cards never expire.

- **Florida.** Cards never expire.

- **Maine.** Cards never expire. If there's less than $5 of value on the card, the store has to give it to you in cash.

- **Massachusetts.** Cards can't expire for seven years. If there's less than $5 of value left on the card, the store has to give it to you in cash. (For *non-reloadable* gift cards, you can get cash for anything that remains under 10 percent of the card's value.)

- **Minnesota.** Cards never expire.

- **Montana.** Cards never expire. If there's less than $5 of value on the card, the store has to give it to you in cash.

- **New Hampshire.** Cards under $100 don't expire. For values over $100, they don't expire for five years.

- **New Jersey.** Cards never expire. If there's less than $5 of value on the card, the store has to give it to you in cash.

- **North Dakota.** Cards don't expire for six years.

- **Rhode Island.** Cards never expire. If there's less than $1 of value on the card, the store has to give it to you in cash.

- **Vermont.** If there's less than $1 of value on the card, the store has to give it to you in cash. After the card has expired, you can get *any* unused value back in cash.

- **Washington.** Cards never expire.

Of course, there's always fine print; for example, these rules usually don't apply to prepaid phone cards or bank cards that you can spend at multiple stores.

But still, all of this should teach you two lessons. First, in your state, your gift card might be even more valuable than you thought.

Second, California's pretty cool.

# The kind of gift card everybody loves

The problem with giving people movie-theater gift cards is that they might not be moviegoers. The problem with giving someone a Starbucks card is that she might not drink coffee. The problem with giving a Macy's card is that there may not be a nearby Macy's.

Here's a little tip: Give your lucky loved one a gift card that's redeemable *anywhere*. Any store, any restaurant. Toward pizza, or plane travel, or paint jobs. Anything.

They're *prepaid Visa cards*. You can get them at drugstores (Walgreens, Rite Aid, Duane Reade, CVS), gas stations (Chevron), convenience stores (7-Eleven, Cumberland Farms), banks (Chase, PNC Bank, U.S. Bank), RadioShack, and grocery stores.

You can also get them online. At GiftCards.com, for example, the card costs $3 or $4 extra, but you can have it printed with a photo of your choice, which makes it a much more personal gift.

(There are also prepaid MasterCards and American Express cards, but they're much less common and harder to find. The AmEx cards are available pretty much only online—at americanexpress.com/gift-cards.)

The beauty of prepaid gift cards is that you can use them just like regular credit cards, to spend wherever you like. They're as universal as cash. (Actually, *more* universal, since you can spend your Visa card on the web, too.) And yet they don't have the impersonal, "I didn't put much effort into this" feel of an envelope full of bills.

They don't expire, and there are no fees.

**Earnings ballpark: The rosy glow of giving a really cool, useful gift**

---

# How to use up the final dollars of a prepaid gift card

Suppose you have a Visa gift card for $50, and you've used up most of it. There's still $4.85 of value left on the card. (How do you know what the card's remaining value is? You call the 800 number on the back.)

And let's say you don't live in one of the states where the store has to give you cash for what's left on the card.

What are you supposed to do—throw away $4.85?

Not at all. Here are several clever ways to wring the last few drips of value from that card.

- **Pay your utility bill with it.** Some gas, electric, cable, and water companies let you pay your bill by credit card. Why not toss that last $4.85 at your bill? Clean and simple.

- **Go out to dinner.** Restaurants routinely let diners split the bill among multiple credit cards. So you can use up what's left on your prepaid card—and pay the rest of the bill with your *real* credit card.

- **Use it up at a big-name store.** At national chains like Target, Whole Foods, and Home Depot, you can split a purchase among multiple credit cards. Swipe your $4.85 gift Visa first; the register applies that amount to your purchase and adjusts the total on the screen. Now pay the remainder with another credit card. (If there's no automated swiping system, you can usually just ask the cashier to do it. That works in gas stations, too.)

- **The classic Amazon-gift-card trick.** Amazon gift cards have two huge advantages. First, you can spend them on anything Amazon sells (which is just about anything ever made). Second, you can buy them in any weird amount—even $4.85.

  So the trick here is to use the remainder of your gift Visa card to buy an Amazon gift card online (which can be just a credit to your own account). Presto: You've converted those money crumbs into a discount on the next thing you buy.

- **Swipe the cards into a Square reader.** You can also convert those leftover card amounts into plain old cash, using a free Square reader, described next.

### Savings ballpark: $30 a year
*$30 = Reclaiming an average of $5 on each of six prepaid Visa cards*

------------------------------------------------------------

# Convert prepaid Visa cards into instant cash

In modern society, prepaid credit cards have become a popular go-to gift for birthdays, Christmas, graduations, and other rites of passage. It's not unusual for a newly minted high school graduate to wind up with a small stack of them.

Wouldn't it be great if you could wave your wand and transform all those cards into money in your bank account, without having to go anywhere or sign anything?

You can—with a Square reader.

A Square card reader is an attachment for an iPhone or Android phone. (You order one from SquareUp.com; it's free.) It plugs into your phone's headphone jack and turns it into a credit card reader. And it lets *anyone* accept credit cards! Kids who mow lawns. Piano teachers. Plumbers. You. Even your teenager.

Square takes 2.75 percent of each credit card swipe and deposits the rest into your bank account. For some people, that's a small price to pay for the ability to eat up stray gift cards—before they get lost in the couch cushions. —*Daniel John Bergsagel*

# Chapter 4:
# House and Home

You already know the common wisdom about saving money on your house. Make sure it's insulated. Use double- or triple-paned windows. Plant shade trees. Save 1 percent on your utility bill for every degree you turn down the thermostat.

But what about some of the lesser known, newer, sneakier ways to keep and save money? That's where this chapter comes in.

-------------------------------------------------------

## How to become a cord-cutter (cable and satellite TV)

The average American cable-TV bill is $100 a month; yours may be much higher. And that's only the beginning; cable and satellite TV service goes up about 8 percent a year, much faster than inflation. Clearly this is an area ripe for finding some savings.

No wonder millions of people every year decide to "cut the cord"—to cancel their cable or satellite service completely.

These days, there are two less expensive ways to get your TV shows and movies. Each involves compromises, and neither is as convenient or complete as a cable subscription. But saving $1,200 a year might help to ease your pain.

**Method 1: Get your TV from the Internet.** Millions of people are perfectly happy to watch the TV shows and movies available from the Internet: Netflix, Hulu, Amazon Video, HBO GO, and so on.

You can watch them on a computer, tablet, or smartphone.

You can also watch them on your actual TV; if you have a fairly recent model, it probably has apps for these services built right in. (So do Blu-ray players and game consoles.) If your TV doesn't offer Netflix, Hulu, and so on, you can always plug into it a "set-top box" like a Roku Streaming Stick ($50), Apple TV ($150), or Chromecast stick ($35; requires a smartphone as a remote control).

These services cost money, but much less than a cable-company package. For example:

- **Netflix ($8 a month)** brings you thousands of old movies and some recent ones, but it also has a gigantic vault of TV shows—complete seasons that finished their run on the big networks: *The Office, Saturday Night Live, Mad Men, The Walking Dead*, and so on. (Netflix's licensing deals are constantly changing, so a TV series or movie that's here now may be gone tomorrow.)

  Netflix also produces its own shows, some of which are outstanding: *House of Cards, Orange Is the New Black*, and so on.

- **Hulu ($8 a month)** offers various network shows online the day after they're broadcast on TV, from ABC, NBC, Bravo, Fox, Comedy Central, Discovery, Nickelodeon, and a few others. Usually, only the most recent handful of episodes are available—not entire seasons, as on Netflix.

  Notably absent: CBS, which offers its own subscription (read on).

- **CBS All Access ($6 a month)** gives you Internet access to most of the stuff broadcast on CBS.

- **Sling TV ($20 a month)** brings you CNN, ESPN, TNT, TBS, Disney, Food Network, ABC Family, Cartoon Network, HGTV, Lifetime, and others.

- **Amazon Prime ($100 a year)** offers thousands of movies, plus the TV shows produced by Amazon itself (*Transparent, Mozart in the Jungle*, and others).

- **HBO NOW ($15 a month)** gets you access to HBO's movies, documentaries, and original series (like *Game of Thrones*).

- **Showtime Anytime ($11 a month)** is your Internet resource for Showtime's movies, boxing matches, and original series.

- **PlayStation Vue ($50 a month)** is an extra-cost feature for Sony's PlayStation game console. It's almost like a little cable box offering CBS, NBC, CNN, Fox, TNT, BET, Comedy Central, Food, HGTV, Syfy, Travel, Animal Planet, and more.

Clearly, no one service offers everything you'd get with a cable package. In fact, once you add up all the services required for the channels you want, you may discover that sticking with cable or satellite winds up being *less* expensive.

Internet TV services, therefore, save money only if you don't want *all* the channels of a cable or satellite package.

**Method 2: Get your TV from an antenna.** In the olden days, everybody got TV channels from an antenna bolted to the roof. Think of all those TV and movie scenes where the hapless suburban dad is on the roof, adjusting the antenna little by little to produce the best picture on the TV in the living room! Now *that's* comedy.

Well, guess what? The TV networks *still* broadcast through the air, and you can *still* tune in to them with an antenna—for free. They come in as great-looking, *full* high-definition signals; they're not compressed, degraded HD signals like the ones you get from cable and satellite. And they bring you live and local broadcasts like sports and news; none of the Internet services listed above carries *live* shows.

You don't have to mount an antenna on the roof anymore, either. The best ones—the ones that tune in the greatest number of channels, from the greatest distance—are still outdoor, roof-mounted models. But plenty of HD antennas are slightly weaker indoor models, designed to sit next to the TV or, preferably, in a window.

You can also install one in your attic, which is a happy medium for many people: The antenna's hidden, it's easy to install, and it's protected from the weather, but it's higher and less wall-blocked than indoor models.

Which stations you'll be able to get depends on where you live. Fortunately, a couple of handy websites let you know which channels you'll get: AntennaWeb.org and TVfool.com. For best results, look this information up *before* you spring for a $60 antenna. (The good news: 89 percent of all U.S. households can tune in to at least five channels over the air like this.)

If you want to *record* shows you get over the air, you'll need a special DVR, like one from Channel Master or TiVo.

Getting going with an HD antenna does require reading some how-to articles online and maybe dedicating an afternoon to installation. But considering the boost in video quality you'll get and the thousands of dollars you'll save every year (by canceling or downgrading your cable subscription), it might be worth a shot.

### Savings ballpark: $1,140 a year
*$1,140 = The average annual cable bill, minus $60 for an HD antenna*

# Free solar panels

We all know that solar power is neato. It's free, it's unlimited, and it's great for the environment. Who could object to a source of power that's as clean and natural as sunshine?

If you live in a sunny climate, you should definitely explore solar, especially since you can get the panels *and* the power they generate at *no cost*.

JON CALLAS

There are two ways to go about getting going with solar. You can buy the solar panels or rent them.

- **Buy the panels.** Solar panels aren't cheap. Depending on the size of your house, you may pay $15,000 to $35,000 to buy and install them. (Loans are available to help you buy the panels.)

  The good news is, though, that you can get nearly half of that back in rebates and tax incentives.

  For example, the IRS will cheerfully refund 30 percent of your solar costs at tax time, thanks to the government's

Residential Renewable Energy Tax Credit. You may get further credits and refunds from your state government, local government, and utility company.

Once the panels are in place, all the power they generate is free. Your house's value goes up.

And this is cool: You can *sell* electricity back to your local power companies. (They love paying you for it, because they're required by law to generate some of their power from renewable sources, like the ones on your roof.) Every time your sunshine generates 1,000 kilowatt-hours of power, you can sell what's called a Solar Renewable Energy Certificate (SREC) to the power company for around $200. You may be able to sell, say, 10 of those annually—a handy $2,000 a year, all thanks to Mother Nature.

Bottom line: In most cases, you'll recoup your expenditure long before the 25-year warranty expires. Free electricity, folks!

You, however, are responsible for any maintenance or repairs that your magic free-energy panels might require. (It's usually not much.)

- **Rent the panels.** Here's where things get exciting: Companies like Sunrun and Sun City would very much like to install solar panels on your roof *for free.* They take care of all the permits, design, repairs, upgrades, and maintenance. They'll even give you a phone app that lets you track how much power your panels are generating and how much money they're saving you.

Why would those companies do something so wonderful for nothing? Are they completely nuts?

Nope. They make money from this. *They* collect all those rebates and incentives for installation, and *they* get to collect all those Solar Renewable Energy Certificates.

They also charge you for electricity. You pay the solar company instead of the electric company, in an arrangement known as a PPA (power purchase agreement).

Fortunately, you pay *less* than you did to the power company, and it's a fixed rate—no surprises each month. (It's usually allowed to creep up annually by a few percent.)

But, meanwhile, you know that you're doing a great thing for the planet, you're saving money, and you've spent $0 to get the system.

If you're tempted by the financial and environmental juiciness of solar but can't decide whether to buy or rent, there's a calculator here that will tell you which approach will save you the most money: energysage.com/market/estimate. (Hint: Owning is usually the better deal, but it requires more work on your part.)

### 20-year savings ballpark:
### $65,000 (own); $27,000 (lease/PPA)

$65,000 = Electricity savings over 20 years in a sunny state
+ value of energy certificates sold + 3 percent home resale value
increase, minus $35,000 cost of installation after rebates
$27,000 = Electricity savings over 20 years for leased solar panels

---------------------------------------------------------------

# Peak and off-peak power:
# When to run the drier

You know about the laws of supply and demand, right? Things always cost more when they're in demand. The cost of a dozen roses doubles around Valentine's Day. Ticket prices at Disney theme parks shoot up on Saturdays and during school holidays. The cost of a ride in an Uber car doubles or triples at rush hour.

Some prices that rise and fall with demand aren't so obvious, however—like electricity.

Most electric companies can sell you power at *tiered* prices— that is, they're willing to charge less during periods of low demand. With these plans, electricity gets cheaper in the evening, and sometimes cheaper yet late at night, like after 9 p.m. (They charge you the most during periods of high demand, like during the workday.)

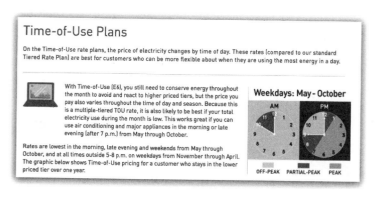

**Time-of-Use Plans**

On the Time-of-Use rate plans, the price of electricity changes by time of day. These rates (compared to our standard Tiered Rate Plan) are best for customers who can be more flexible about when they are using the most energy in a day.

With Time-of-Use (E6), you still need to conserve energy throughout the month to avoid and react to higher priced tiers, but the price you pay also varies throughout the time of day and season. Because this is a multiple-tiered TOU rate, it is also likely to be best if your total electricity use during the month is low. This works great if you can use air conditioning and major appliances in the morning or late evening (after 7 p.m.) from May through October.

Rates are lowest in the morning, late evening and weekends from May through October, and at all times outside 5-8 p.m. on weekdays from November through April. The graphic below shows Time-of-Use pricing for a customer who stays in the lower priced tier over one year.

**Weekdays: May - October**

OFF-PEAK   PARTIAL-PEAK   PEAK

If you're not even home during the day, you may as well take advantage of these plans and start saving money. That involves three steps:

- **Find out what your utility's time-of-day plan is.** Call them, or visit their website. In most states, the plans are similar to that of PG&E (California's utility, the country's largest electric company): If you're on their standard time-of-day plan, you'll discover that the price of power jumps up by about 25 percent between 3 and 9 p.m., when most people are home.

- **Switch to the time-of-day plan.** For most electric companies, the time-of-day plan is one of several options; you have to request it.

- **Save power and money.** Some of your home's biggest electricity gulpers run all the time (like refrigerators and water heaters), so there's not much you can do about *when* they run. But other power hounds are within your control.

After heating and cooling, the biggest consumer of electricity in your home is your clothes drier. Every load of clothes you wash and dry costs you about $1 in power. Well, guess what? It's easy enough to run your washer and drier after 9 p.m.

Same goes for your dishwasher, vacuum cleaner, dehumidifier, and electric car. If you can run or charge them after 9 p.m. (or in the morning), you save 25 percent.

### Savings ballpark: $125 a year

*$125 = $70 savings on running the drier (6.7 kW per load, two loads a week, 10 cents off-peak) + $29 savings on washing machine (2.75 kW per load, two loads a week, 10 cents off-peak) + 5 kW for miscellaneous other devices off-peak*

-----------------------------------------------------------

# The LED lightbulb revolution

What is *wrong* with people? If they had any idea how great LED lightbulbs are, they'd never buy any other kind of bulb again.

LED bulbs turn on to full brightness instantly. They remain cool to the touch. They're hard to break and safety-coated if they do. They work in the cold and in high humidity. They put out negligible heat.

Above all—since you've gone to the trouble of picking up a book about money—LED bulbs save you money, hand over fist. In two ways:

- **70 percent lower lighting bill.** Incandescent bulbs are incredibly inefficient; they burn up 90 percent of their energy as heat, not light. No wonder an LED bulb needs only 30 percent as much juice. In other words, LED bulbs mean lower utility bills and a *much* smaller carbon footprint for your home.

- **20 times longer life.** LED bulbs last 20 years or more. Yes, they cost more than traditional bulbs: maybe $5 for a 100-watt equivalent, vs. $1 for an incandescent bulb. But practically speaking, you'll buy a new *house* before you have to buy a new LED bulb.

LED bulbs also contain electronics, a fact that has sent clever inventors into overdrive. You can buy bulbs that change color, that contain wireless speakers, that turn themselves on and off

on a schedule automatically. And you can control it all with a smartphone app.

The old concerns about LED bulbs' color and dimmability have long since been addressed. You can now buy them at whatever "color temperature" (color tone) you want, and the package lets you know which ones are dimmable.

The sooner you replace your house's bulbs with LED, the sooner you'll start saving money—and seeing better.

### 10-year savings ballpark: $900 in electricity, $60 in bulb replacements

$900 = 10-year electricity savings for 12 bulbs ($11 per year per incandescent bulb running four hours daily, with electricity at 11 cents per kWh, minus $3.50 for an LED bulb)
$60 = 10-year bulb savings (a dozen incandescents every year at $1 each, minus one set of 12 $5 LED bulbs)

---

# Reusable gift wrap: Like money in your bank

Must be nice to be in the gift-wrap business. You're selling rolls of very cheap paper at a satisfying markup. It's made to be used only once and then ripped up and thrown away. At that point, people have only one choice: to buy more.

There are three annoying aspects to this cycle. First, you have to keep buying this stuff. Second, it's a fussy, time-consuming job to use it—to wrap up the presents with it. Third, it's not always a joyride for the recipient to *open* the package ("Can you hand me the scissors?").

Why do we wrap gifts, anyway? To conceal what's inside until the big day of opening, of course. To preserve the surprise, preferably with an eye-catching and festive look.

So here's the idea: Instead of buying rolls of gift-wrap paper every year, buy a set of gift-wrap *bags*. They look just like wrapping paper (they're printed with the same cheerful decorative patterns), but they're drawstring bags. Draw-*ribbon* bags, actually. You can get about 60 of them, in sizes from tiny to enormous, for $12.

Suddenly, your wrapping job is nearly instantaneous—you just drop the present into the bag and draw it tight with the ribbon handles. The result looks just like a regular wrapped gift, but it's much easier to open.

And here's the beautiful part: You don't throw it away. You reuse the same 60 bags, year after year. You're doing a good deed for your time, your recipients' time, the environment— and your wallet.

### Savings ballpark: $15 a year
$15 = Three rolls of wrapping paper at $5 each, enough
to cover eight gifts for four people annually

# Dry your hands the 1890s way

According to legend, the Scott Paper Co. of Philadelphia invented paper towels by accident.

At the time, Scott was in the business of making *toilet* paper. But then, one fateful day in 1907, a railroad car arrived at the plant, full of paper that was too thick to serve as T.P.

Co-founder Arthur Scott didn't want to throw away all that raw material. So he cut it into squares and sold it to hotels and restaurants as a hygienic, disposable alternative to cloth towels in public restrooms.

To this day, paper towels are great for mopping up spills that are too gross for wiping up with a sponge—pet messes, for example.

They are not, however, any better than cloth hand towels for *drying your hands.*

The old argument against hand towels—the one that Arthur Scott had in mind—is that they spread germs from one hand-wiper to another. But these days, who needs to dry their hands? People who have *just washed them!* Their hands are already clean!

The bottom line: If you learn to dry your hands on a *hand* towel after washing them, rather than ripping off a square of paper towel every time, you'll help both your bank account and the environment.

### Savings ballpark: $85 a year
$85 = One roll of paper towels saved each week at $1.75 per roll, minus $6 Walmart hand-towel set

# Free fine art
# for your fine walls

Fine art is usually considered a wealthy person's game. A handsome original piece of art might cost hundreds or thousands of dollars, plus $300 to get it custom-framed.

There is, however, an ingenious way to get stunning artwork for nothing—and to custom-frame it for one-tenth as much as you'd expect.

- **Step 1: Get the free art.** Visit Flickr.com, one of the Internet's largest repositories for spectacular photography. Search for the kind of imagery you're looking for: *landscape, cityscape, trees, sunset, abstract,* whatever. (Bonus tip: Search *spiral staircases.* Those make really cool art, especially in black and white.)

The search will unearth thousands of images that match your description. Now you want to find the *free* ones—the ones whose creators have already given permission for anyone to use their work in any way.

To do that, click the "Any license" pop-up menu and choose "All creative commons." Now you're looking at pictures that you're free to download and print.

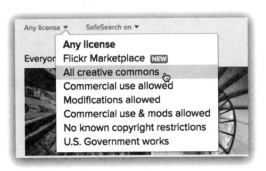

(By the way: If you see an image you love that instead says "All rights reserved," feel free to email the photographer and explain what you have in mind. Offer something—maybe $20. As long as you're not using that picture for *commercial* use, like in an advertisement, you'll usually get an OK.)

Click the photo and inspect it; make sure that its resolution will be high enough for the print size you want. If its dimensions are in the mid-thousands (for example, 5472 × 2648 pixels), you'll be in good shape.

Download the file.

- **Step 2: Order the framed print.** A number of websites offer professional printing and framing of any picture you send them. At mpix.com, for example, you can upload your photo, choose a frame type, specify a final size, and order the whole thing. They'll print the photo on gorgeous paper and frame it for you in a couple of days. An 8-by-10-inch photo becomes an 11½-by-13½-inch framed print—and costs about $26.

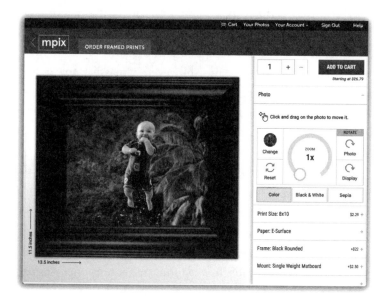

The final results look *exactly* like the most professional, high-end photography and framing you could possibly buy. Nobody will ever know that your grand total expenditure was 26 bucks.

### Savings ballpark: $474 per framed print
*$474 = $200 commercial artwork, custom-framed for $300, minus the cost of a Flickr print, printed and framed for $26*

# Cool breeze on, air conditioner off

The air conditioner is a marvel, isn't it? Our sweltering ancestors, toiling indoors in the steamy summer heat, would have fallen down and worshipped it as a god.

The air conditioner is also, however, a massive power hog. During periods of great summer hotness, its appetite can account for *half* your electric bill. No other appliance comes even close. (Air conditioners alone consume 5 percent of all the electricity in America.)

Exactly how much it costs to run the AC depends on the size of your house, the power of the unit, the temperature and humidity outside, the setting you've dialed up, the current price of electricity, and so on. But just for kicks, here's a typical example: A central air conditioner using 900 kilowatt-hours a month will cost you $120 a month. A window air conditioner running six hours a day (270 kilowatt-hours) will cost $35 a month.

If you're not the only one at home—if you're sharing the space with other hot people—then running the AC makes sense.

But if it's just you sitting at a desk, or you and another person sleeping in a bed, then a *fan* is an enormous money saver. It can keep you comfortable, but it costs you next to nothing. Maybe a penny an hour.

(A fan cools you in two ways: By pushing your own body heat away from your skin and by evaporating the sweat off your skin, which has a cooling effect.)

A ceiling fan set on high, running for 12 hours a day, will cost you maybe $3.50 a month—that's *one-tenth* as much as a window air conditioner, or *3 percent* as much as central air. A desk fan, of course, saves even more.

And when it's too hot for a fan to do the job—when the room air is above 85 degrees, for example—use the fan *and* the air conditioner. You'll be able to set the AC to a higher temp, running it less, and rely on the fan to make up the difference.

## Savings ballpark: $226 a year

$226 = Central air at $120 per month, minus ceiling fan at $3.50 per month, running four months a year and reducing central air use by half

---

# The embarrassing truth about programmable thermostats

You don't need an engineering degree to see how a programmable thermostat saves money.

A manual, dumb thermostat wastes an insane amount of energy by heating or cooling your house *when there's nobody in it.* That makes about as much sense as running an empty oven. Or mowing a parking lot.

A programmable thermostat, of course, is one that you set to run during specific times of day. It warms or cools the house only when you're *there* and saves money the rest of the time.

But here's an astonishing statistic: Only 30 percent of U.S. thermostats are programmable. And of those, fewer than half are actually programmed! According to a Berkeley National Laboratory study, 53 percent of us just set the thing to one temperature and then hit Hold!

We turn our smart thermostats into dumb ones and pointlessly burn hundreds of dollars a year.

Yes, that's appalling, but you can't blame the homeowners. First of all, most of us don't choose our thermostats; they are already on the wall when we move in.

Worse, the thermostats themselves are about as easy to operate as a Boeing 747. Quick: What's the difference between Temporary Override, Timed Hold, Permanent Hold, Permanent Override, and Away modes?

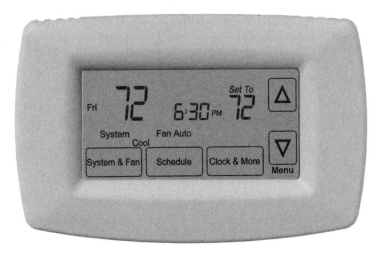

Most thermostats are just too hard to figure out. And the manuals probably disappeared sometime around the Reagan administration.

Still, fixing the thermostat situation in your home is hugely important. According to the U.S. Department of Energy, programming your thermostat correctly can save 15 percent on your heating bill. In an average home, that's a savings of $100 (natural gas) to $315 (oil) every winter. In the summer, you'll save another $75 or so on air conditioning.

All right. So let's suppose you have a manual thermostat, or a programmable one that's too hard to figure out. Take a deep breath, set aside a Saturday, and proceed like this:

- **If you have a programmable thermostat but lost the manual:** Somewhere on that thing, you'll find a sticker or a panel that tells you the brand and model. Go to Google and search for its user guide. Type, for example, *Honeywell RTH6450D1009 manual.*

Sure enough: You'll find that the instruction manual is available to read online, or to download and print. Invite a neighborhood teenager to stand by your side, if necessary, and force yourself to program that thermostat.

Set it to allow the house to cool down (in winter) or heat up (in summer) during the hours when nobody's home—and when you're asleep on a different floor.

• **If you don't have a programmable thermostat:** Get one. They cost as little as $25. (If you're handy with a screwdriver and can follow instructions online, you can install it yourself. Otherwise, factor in an electrician visit.)

Anything you buy today will be easier to use than the user-hostile designs of 10 years ago. But if you have a smartphone (like an iPhone or an Android phone), you'll get particular joy out of a Nest thermostat or Honeywell Lyric thermostat. The Nest programs *itself* by learning the patterns of your daily comings and goings; the Lyric detects when you're approaching or leaving home (from the GPS of your phone) and heats or cools the house accordingly. You can operate either one by remote control, using an app on your phone.

These amazing thermostats cost $200 or $240—which you'll recoup in just over a year.

### Savings ballpark: $280 a year
$280 = Annual savings in heat and cooling by programming the thermostat—a nice, even number between $175 (savings if you have gas heat) and $390 (oil heat)

# Instructions for boiling water

Time for tea! Or soup! Or pasta! Or lobster!

But what's the best way to boil the water?

You could put the kettle on the stove. You could use an electric kettle that doesn't *require* a stove. You could microwave a cup of water. You could start with hot water from your faucet and heat it up from there.

Here's the answer, as determined by the number crunchers at TreeHugger.com:

- **Worst way: the stove.** A lot of heat gets wasted as it travels from the flames (or electric coil) to the metal of the kettle or pot, and from there to the water. You're also heating a lot of air around the pot. Time: 5 minutes. Efficiency: 30 percent.

- **Better: the microwave.** The nice part here is that you're heating only the water and the mug. (You waste some power by heating the mug, but of course the mug will then keep your water hot longer.) Time: 3 minutes. Efficiency: 47 percent.

- **Best: an electric kettle.** The heating element is in direct contact with the water, so you're not heating anything that you don't need to heat. And the thing shuts off when your water is boiling. Time: 2 minutes. Efficiency: 81 percent.

Starting with hot water from your faucet doesn't really count for much either way; you've already used power to heat it up.

**Savings ballpark: $2.50 a year
+ deep satisfaction**

$2.50 = 0.07 kWh of electricity saved per boiling (0.11 kWh for the stove, 0.04 kWh for the kettle) × 12 cents per kWh average electricity price × two boilings a day × 365

---

# The "It takes more energy to reheat a room" myth: Demolished

When it comes time to program your thermostat, you may be haunted by the memory of some friend or parent saying: "It's cheaper to keep the heat on all night! Because if you let the downstairs get cold, it takes more energy to reheat it in the morning."

As it turns out, that's false. It takes *less* energy to bring a cold room back up to 68 degrees than it does to keep it there all night.

---

# The "heat the house faster" myth: Demolished

Surely you've seen them: people who think they can get the house warmed up faster if they set the temp *beyond* the comfort point. In other words, you like 68 degrees in winter, but you come downstairs to a 64-degree room—so you set the thermostat to 85 to make it heat up faster.

In fact, you'll only waste power and money that way. Heating is either on or off, like a light switch. The room warms up at the same rate, whether you set the thermostat to 68, 100, or 5,000 degrees.

So set it to 68 and be patient.

(All of this applies equally to air conditioning. And the same principle also applies in your car.)

---------------------------------------------------------------

# The replacement-window myth: Demolished

The ads aren't shy. They make it explicitly clear that if you replace old, drafty windows with modern, energy-efficient ones, you'll save a lot of energy and money.

Well, that's true. But window replacements aren't cheap; upgrading all your windows can cost thousands of dollars.

Replacing your windows makes sense if you're aiming to solve environmental, cosmetic, or draftiness problems. If you're planning to replace windows anyway, definitely get high-efficiency ones.

But if you're considering making that move purely as a financial play, you may be making a mistake. According to energy experts, there are many less expensive moves you should make first.

For example, you'll get a giant energy savings just by sealing gaps around doors, windows, pipe cutouts, and other transitions to the outdoors. (A home energy checkup, or energy audit, is often worthwhile; read on.)

**Savings ballpark: $7,000**
$7,000 = Cost of 15 vinyl-clad windows, installed, at $500 each, minus $500 for an energy audit

- - - - - - - - - - - - - - - - - - - - - - - - - - - - - - - - - - - - - - - - -

# The light-switch myth: Demolished

Here's something else some family member or co-worker might have mentioned to you: "Stop turning the light off all the time. It uses more energy to turn it off and on all the time than to just leave it on."

Turns out that's not true. No matter what kind of bulb, turning the light off whenever possible saves energy—and money.

- - - - - - - - - - - - - - - - - - - - - - - - - - - - - - - - - - - - - - - - -

# In praise of the home energy audit

Your house is equipped with big machines that pump heated or cooled air into its rooms, but the house itself is a leaky vessel. Usually, anywhere from 5 to 30 percent of that heated or cooled air leaks out of the house.

In other words, unless your house was built recently, the odds are very good that you're spending a huge amount to heat or cool the *outdoors*. You're ensuring comfort for the birds and the bees, along with your family.

Identifying the cracks, holes, and leaky spots is one of the primary goals of an energy audit or energy checkup. If heating and cooling were minor expenses in your life, this kind of headache wouldn't be worth it. But home energy is a *huge* expense—and an audit *is* worth it.

You can do the inspection yourself, if you've got more time than money. Your own government has posted a handy guide at energy.gov/energysaver/do-it-yourself-home-energy-audits.

That page tells you what to look for: gaps along the baseboards and wall joints, missing insulation, and so on.

If you're willing to invest a few hundred bucks, though, it's much better to hire a professional to do this job, someone who's equipped with detection equipment like infrared scanners to spot the heat leaks. In theory, you'll recoup the expense of the energy audit fairly quickly once your leaky house is patched up.

To find an energy auditor, you have a few options:

- Visit resnet.us/directory/search.

- Ask your electric or gas company. They can often recommend local firms—or even offer a discounted or free audit themselves.

- Ask the energy or sustainability office for your town or state. (Yes, you have one. Google *cleveland energy office,* for example.)

### Savings ballpark: $1,000 a year
*$1,000 = Typical annual heating, cooling, and electric savings to result from energy-audit findings*

# Never get ripped off on home services again

You need a painter, electrician, plumber, architect, or construction contractor. You want someone to mow your lawn, clean your gutters, or babysit your kid. You wonder which is the best electricity supplier, Internet provider, or cable TV company. Where do you start?

All these service industries are teeming with companies that might disappoint you. And those services are expensive, so you probably want to avoid hiring a deadbeat.

Where do you go for such local advice? Here are three ways to find it:

- **Yelp.com** is the Internet's biggest database of reviews for local businesses—20 million of them. Almost every service, store, and restaurant gets reviewed by actual customers and

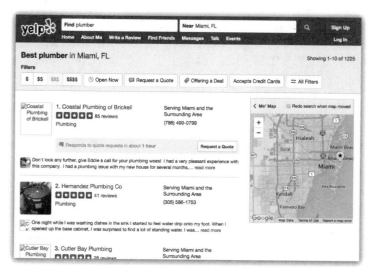

gets a star rating for easy comparison. And Yelp is free to everyone.

The only downside of searching Yelp is that, because it's so free and open, some of these businesses try to game the system. They post positive reviews about themselves under fake names, for example. Yelp has a huge fraud team (and clever software algorithms) dedicated to weeding out such phonies, but they can't catch them all; you have to use your own judgment.

• **Angie's List.** From its founding in 1995, this massive database of customer reviews and ratings (AngiesList.com) was a subscription-only service costing around $30 a year. Now, happily, it's free to everyone.

This site is better controlled, organized, and cleaned up than Yelp; customers rate each service on its professionalism, price, quality, and responsiveness and then give it a grade, A to F.

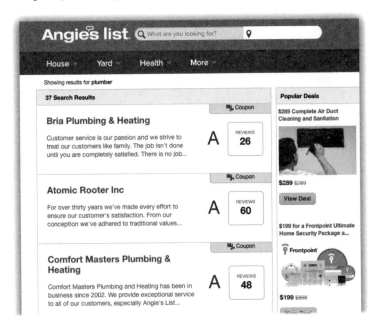

- **Nextdoor.com.** Here's a fantastic free site that's been hiding right under your nose. Nextdoor is a *hyper*-local bulletin board—that is, you're hearing from people who live not just in your town, but on your own *block.*

The posts include plenty of "Has anyone seen my dog?" and "Anyone want an old couch?" messages, but there are also a lot of "Who knows of a good snow-plowing service?" and "Anyone know a reasonably priced mechanic?" posts. Almost always, you get prompt responses from people who've been down your road before.

**Savings ballpark: Months of headache**

- - - - - - - - - - - - - - - - - - - - - - - - - - - - - - - - - - - - - - - -

# How not to get ripped off on Valentine's Day roses

Florists aren't crazy. They know perfectly well when everyone in the world is going to want red roses: February 14. Valentine's Day.

No wonder the price of red roses spikes dramatically during that week. It usually *doubles*.

But information is money—and here's the information you need to fight back.

- **Buy them before the spike.** Roses usually last five days before they wilt. But they can last much longer if you're smart.

  Trim their stems when they arrive. Change the water every couple of days. Keep them away from heat and windows.

  Finally, the big one: Put the stems in sugar water (6 teaspoons of sugar in 32 ounces of water). That simple act gives roses three more days of life, meaning that you can buy them as early as February 9 and avoid the red-rose rush hour.

  But the real miracle drug is *silver nitrate*—a chemical related to what people used to use to develop film. You can buy a bottle for $20 online. Add a few drops to the roses' water, and you can extend their life *another* four days. (Lawyers' note: Don't drink or touch silver nitrate.)

- **Choose other colors.** Red roses cost around $20 more per dozen than pink, yellow, or orange ones. Would your beloved be insulted if the roses weren't red?

- **Go for the bouquet.** Order a bouquet that includes roses *and* other flowers. For the price of a dozen roses, you can get a truly spectacular spring bouquet that actually provides a much stronger, lovelier fragrance than commercial roses alone.

- **Buy the roses online.** Services like ProFlowers.com and TheBouqs.com sell roses at lower prices than local shops do, in part because they send the roses directly from the rose farms.

In fact, if you're willing to accept delivery a few days before February 14, you can save as much as 25 percent.

Bonus tip: It's easy to find coupon codes for online florists; do a quick search at RetailMeNot.com (page 16).

Finally, of course, there's the nuclear option: Buy your roses on February 15, the day *after* Valentine's Day. You lose some romance points, but you get gorgeous roses dirt cheap—and you save enough to take your beloved out to a really nice dinner.

### Savings ballpark: $40 a year
*$40 = Savings on 12 long-stemmed roses delivered
on February 9 or 15, instead of February 14*

# Chapter 5:
# Tech and TV

We love us our gadgets. They keep us entertained, keep us in touch, keep us informed.

They also keep us paying through the nose. Cable TV, Internet, and cell phone service—and the electronics we use to access them—have come to represent an enormous chunk of our expenditures these days.

They are, therefore, ripe for inspection by the ardent money-saver.

-----------------------------------------------------------------

# Where to buy
# new tech for cheap

Every computer manufacturer's website offers a listing of *refurbished* machines at huge discounts. You'll find special pages listing this equipment on the websites of Apple, Dell, HP, and so on. (To find these special pages, use Google to search, for example, for *refurbished Macs* or *refurbished Dell*.)

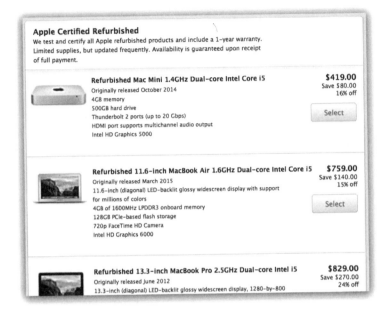

**Apple Certified Refurbished**
We test and certify all Apple refurbished products and include a 1-year warranty. Limited supplies, but updated frequently. Availability is guaranteed upon receipt of full payment.

**Refurbished Mac Mini 1.4GHz Dual-core Intel Core i5**
Originally released October 2014
4GB memory
500GB hard drive
Thunderbolt 2 ports (up to 20 Gbps)
HDMI port supports multichannel audio output
Intel HD Graphics 5000

**$419.00**
Save $80.00
16% off

[ Select ]

**Refurbished 11.6-inch MacBook Air 1.6GHz Dual-core Intel Core i5**
Originally released March 2015
11.6-inch (diagonal) LED-backlit glossy widescreen display with support for millions of colors
4GB of 1600MHz LPDDR3 onboard memory
128GB PCIe-based flash storage
720p FaceTime HD Camera
Intel HD Graphics 6000

**$759.00**
Save $140.00
15% off

[ Select ]

**Refurbished 13.3-inch MacBook Pro 2.5GHz Dual-core Intel i5**
Originally released June 2012
13.3-inch (diagonal) LED-backlit glossy widescreen display, 1280-by-800

**$829.00**
Save $270.00
24% off

Now, your first instinct might be to exclaim: "Eww! I don't want some used computer, full of cat hair and baby drool!"

Ah, but in this case, the "refurbished" computers aren't what you'd expect. They're brand-new. They haven't been used. They've been inspected even more thoroughly than new machines. And they have the same warranty.

Usually, they were bought and then returned for some reason, sometimes without even being opened.

For your willingness to buy something that's been shipped and returned, you're treated to substantial price cuts. Keep this trick in mind the next time you're in the market for a new laptop, tablet, or whatever.

### Savings ballpark: $250

*$250 = Savings on a 13-inch MacBook Air,*
*$1,200 new, offered at $950 refurbished*

# Cheaper cable TV through creative cord-cutting calls

Cord-cutting. It's happening all over the country, and it's freaking out the cable companies.

Cord-cutting means canceling your TV service. To paraphrase millions of people everywhere: "Why should I pay $180 a month for a bunch of channels I never watch? I can get the good shows directly from the Internet—Netflix, Hulu, iTunes, and so on." (See page 67 for more on cord-cutting.)

The thing is, the cable/satellite companies spent a *lot* of money on marketing to get you to sign up in the first place—at least $1,000 per customer. And in this day of Internet TV, it's getting harder and harder to sign up new customers. So they'll bend over backward, financially speaking, to stop you from canceling.

So here's what you do:

- **Call your cable or satellite company.** Tell the customer service rep that you'd like to cancel your service.

   (Note: If you don't have the nerve to bluff like this, simply say that you want to cut your service down to the *most basic* plan. That way, you're not bluffing. If it actually comes to that, and they change your plan, no harm done. Just call up the next day and restore your higher-priced plan.)

   (Another note: If you don't even have enough nerve to do *that,* you can often have good luck just calling and *asking* for a better deal—without threatening to quit or downgrade. Especially if you've been a customer for a long time, you might be surprised at how willing the cable company might be to help you out. —*James Dietsch*)

- **They'll ask you why you want to cancel.** Tell them you've decided to cut the cord: You're happy getting your TV from Netflix and Hulu.

- **The rep will probably transfer you** to the Customer Retention Group or a customer loyalty agent. This is a special department that exists solely to stop people from canceling.

- **The retention specialist** will offer to lower your bill if you're willing to change your mind about canceling.

- **The more you insist** on canceling anyway, the better the offer.

  If you've read about a better deal from a rival cable or satellite company, by all means mention what it is. Insist that you'll remain a customer only if the rep can match that deal.

What kind of deal will you get? It depends on your persistence and what kind of plan you're already on. Maybe you'll get $40 a month knocked off your bill. Or, if you already pay for TV *and* Internet (or TV, Internet, and phone service) from a single company, the deal might be so good that you get the TV service for almost nothing.

### Savings ballpark: $480 a year
*$480 = $40 negotiated discount from your monthly bill*

---

# Buy your own cable box, save hundreds

As though the cable companies weren't already milking you dry with the cost of the TV service, they're also charging you about $235 a year to *rent the cable box* (the one that changes channels and connects to your TV). It's about $7.50 a month per box. Most people have more than one TV, so they rent more than one cable box.

If your cable box also includes a video recorder (DVR), you're paying even more. Now you're talking $300 or $400 a year.

As it turns out, it's 100 percent OK to supply your *own* cable box or DVR and eliminate those expenses!

The best of the best is the TiVo, which is both a cable box and a DVR. (Some TiVo models require you to pay a monthly fee [$15] or a one-time, lifetime service payment [$250].)

But at sites like CableBoxandModem.com, you can buy your own replacement cable box for $120 (pays for itself in 16 months) or a combination cable box/DVR for $200 (pays for itself in eight months—no service fees).

Now, part of the purpose of a cable box is security; the cable company wants to make sure you're actually paying for all the channels you're receiving. If you supply your own cable box, how will your cable company know it's you?

Because you'll slip a CableCard into it. You can buy a Cable-Card for under $5 from the cable company, preprogrammed with your account information, and slip it into the back of the box you've bought.

(By the way: When you call the cable company to request that they send you a CableCard, don't let them play dumb. They are legally obligated to sell you one and even help you install it.)

### Savings ballpark: $192 a year
$192 = Savings of $10 a month for each of two cable boxes, minus rental of two CableCards for $2 per month

---

# Don't pay for cable while you're away

If you go away for vacation—or if you spend your time in two different homes during the year—why should you have to pay for cable TV or satellite service while you're away? You shouldn't!

Unbeknownst to almost everybody, the cable and satellite companies offer vacation-suspension plans. All you have to do is call to let them know when you're leaving and when you're returning—and then stop paying while you're away!

The plans may change over time, but here are some examples:

- **Comcast Xfinity** (800-934-6489). *How long can you suspend?* Three to nine months. *How often?* Once a year. *How much does it cost?* $7 a month each for TV and Internet. *Notes:* The program, called Vacation Hold, is available only in Indiana, Michigan, Chicago, and Florida.

- **Time Warner** (800-892-4357). *How long can you suspend?* Two to 10 months. *How often?* Once a year. *How much does it cost?* $5 a month.

- **Dish** (844-394-6568). *How long can you suspend?* Two to nine months. *How often?* Once a year. *How much does it cost?* $5 a month.

- **DirecTV** (800-507-2716). *How long can you suspend?* One to six months. *How often?* Twice a year. *How much does it cost?* No charge.

- **AT&T U-verse TV** (800-288-2020). *How long can you suspend?* One to two months. *How often?* Once a year. *How much does it cost?* $17 a month.

- **Verizon Fios** (800-300-4184). *How long can you suspend?* One to nine months. *How often?* As often as you like. *How much does it cost?* $40 per suspension.

- **Cox Communications** (866-961-0027). *How long can you suspend?* One month to forever. *How often?* Twice a year. *How much does it cost?* $20 a month.

- **Charter Spectrum** (800-398-6192). *How long can you suspend?* Up to six months. *How often?* Once a year. *How much does it cost?* $12 to $15 a month per service (TV, Internet, phone).

**Savings ballpark: $285 a year**
$285 = Average U.S. $100 cable bill suspended
for three months, minus $5 monthly fee

---

# Supply your own cable modem

It's bad enough that your cable company makes you rent the cable box that plugs into your TV. At this moment, you're also paying to rent your cable *modem,* the gadget that brings

high-speed Internet into your house. This time, the damage is about $10 a month, forever.

Once again, there's no reason for you to keep paying! Buy your own cable modem for $100, return the one you've been renting, and boom: a $120-a-year savings.

Before you shop for your own modem, make sure you've found one that works with your cable company. Do a Google search for, for example, *comcast compatible modems.*

Once you've ordered the modem, call up the cable company and let them know you've bought your own (which is perfectly OK and increasingly common). They'll walk you through setting it up. They'll give you the address of a return center for shipping back the one you've been renting.

And then they'll take that $10 fee off your monthly bill!

**Savings ballpark: $120 a year**
*$120 = Savings of $10-per-month cable-modem rental every year*

---

# Driving a stake through vampire power

We leave all kinds of things plugged in when we're not using them: microwaves, game consoles, TVs, cell phone chargers, computers, cable modems, cable boxes, garage-door openers. Unfortunately, all those things keep using electricity, even when they're in idle, standby, or sleep mode. They stay on so that their clocks or status gauges remain up to date, so that they turn on quickly when we want them, or so that they can remain "listening" for signals from a remote control.

The trickle of juice they keep using is called vampire power. (Why? Because vampires are invisible and they suck the life out of us. Get it?)

American households spend about $19 billion a year on vampire power. Your share: $165 a year on average, $400 a year if you have a high-tech kind of house.

A big part of the problem is that many household appliances that were once purely mechanical now have screens, Internet connections, and other digital elements: washers, driers, toasters, microwaves, refrigerators, and so on. So they consume a trickle of power all the time.

In any case, vampire power costs you, and it costs the earth. America's vampire power alone consumes the output equivalent of 50 large power plants.

According to the Natural Resources Defense Council, here are the steps you can take to fight back:

- **Unplug things that don't need to be on,** like the TV, cable box, and DVR in the guest room, the furnace in the summertime, or a second refrigerator. (If you can get rid of the second fridge altogether, that's even better; older fridges, like the ones people keep in their garages or basements, use old, juice-guzzling technology.)

- **Use smart power strips.** You can plug all your TV stuff (set, speakers, Blu-ray player) into a single strip, and turn them on or off all at once when you need them. Same thing with your computer system: PC, monitor, printer, speakers.

In fact, because so many people are trying to clamp down on vampire power, you can now buy *smart* power strips. Some

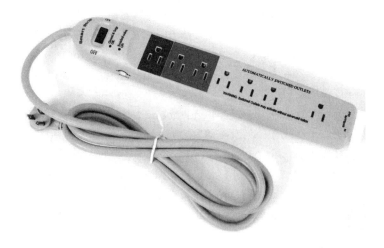

use a master-slave arrangement: If you turn off the main appliance (like the computer), then the associated outlets (like the monitor and printer) also cut power.

To find these strips, do a Google search for *smart power strip*.

• **Automatically limit the charging time.** For about $6.50, you can get a Belkin Conserve Socket (or one of its rivals). It cuts off power automatically after 30 minutes, three hours, or six hours—perfect for phones, tablets, laptops, and other things that you plug in to recharge. There's really no point in letting them suck up juice after they're fully charged; in fact, most manufacturers suggest *not* leaving them plugged in all the time.

• **Use timed outlets.** Some power strips (and power-outlet adapters) are programmable. You can set them up to cut power based on time of day (do a Google search for *timed power strip*), which is perfect for gadgets like water recirculation pumps, coffeemakers, towel heaters, and heated bathroom floors.

• **Turn off the instant-on feature.** Most TVs are on even when they're off. They remain in "instant on" mode so that they'll pop right to life when you hit the On button on the remote. Same thing for game consoles.

The thing is, you can turn that feature *off* on many models (burrow into the settings). If you don't use your TV or console every day, it might be worth the trade-off: You'll have to wait a minute for the thing to warm up when you turn it on, but you won't be guzzling juice all day and night.

**Savings ballpark: $165 a year**
*$165 = The per-household amount of the $19 billion a year Americans spend on vampire power, according to the Natural Resources Defense Council*

- - - - - - - - - - - - - - - - - - - - - - - - - - - - - - - - - - - - - - - - - - - - - - -

# The Great Digital-Cable Scam

For decades, audio nuts have debated the value of buying absurdly expensive cables to connect their stereo components. Surely *gold-tipped* cables must conduct sound more purely and authentically than cables made of more ordinary stuff.

Well, no book author would be wise to step onto *that* battleground. Judging sound is a black art, highly subjective—a world where there's no clear right or wrong.

*Digital* cables, however, are a different story.

These days, the cable that carries audio and video between TV components is called HDMI. It's the one that connects TVs to Blu-ray players, cable boxes, Apple TVs, TiVos, and other gear.

Monster Gold Advanced High Speed HDMI Cable with Ethernet - 12 ft.
by Monster
★★★★★ ▾    6 customer reviews
Price: $58.39 & **FREE Shipping**
Only 7 left in stock.
Length: **12 Feet**

The makers of cables have eagerly jumped into the market with the same marketing message they've always used for audio. They want you to believe that fancy gold- or even platinum-tipped HDMI cables will give you better picture and sound. They hope to exploit the same sort of uncertainty that's allowed them to profit from audio cables for years.

Unfortunately for them, there *is* no uncertainty this time. An HDMI cable carries nothing but digital signals—1's and 0's, the language of computers. There's no such thing as an HDMI cable whose signal looks *a little better* than another; an HDMI cable either works completely or doesn't work at all.

Therefore, a $7 HDMI cable you buy online is just as good as an $80 HDMI cable from your local TV store.

### Savings ballpark: $146
*$146 = Savings of $73 off each of two gold-tipped HDMI cables*

-------------------------------------------------

# Cell phone service for $8 a month—or even free

What you're currently paying for cell phone service is probably around $75 a month; that's the average American cell phone bill. Actually, nearly half of us pay over *$100* a month.

Well, how'd you like to pay less than *one-twelfth* that much? Or even get your service for nothing?

You can—by using a *prepaid* plan. Instead of paying the carrier at the end of the month, you buy minutes and data *before* you use them. (It's really not such a strange setup; your car is on a prepaid plan, too. You pay for the gas before you use it.)

In the beginning, prepaid phones came from little companies that, behind the scenes, bought and resold cellular bandwidth from the Big Four (Verizon, AT&T, Sprint, and T-Mobile). You might have been paying a company called Red Pocket, but behind the scenes, it was AT&T carrying your calls and getting you online.

These days, the Big Four have bought up a lot of those little companies, to capitalize on the growing popularity of prepaid plans. You may have heard of Cricket Wireless (owned by AT&T), Boost Mobile and Virgin Mobile USA (Sprint), GoSmart Mobile and MetroPCS (T-Mobile), or Page Plus Cellular (Verizon). Each Big Four company also offers prepaid plans under its own name.

In addition to saving you all kinds of money, prepaid phones have a bunch of other advantages. There's no contract; you can stop and start service whenever you like. There's no monthly bill. There's no "activation fee," that stupid $35 that the Big Four charge every time you start service. There's no credit check or age limit, either, which is what makes prepaid phones useful to con men and con children.

So how much can you save by paying in advance? A ton. The exact prices and offerings will have changed by the time you reach the end of this sentence, but the following examples are typical.

Remember: The point of comparison is what the average American spends on cell phone service a month—$75—on the traditional (postpaid) plan.

- **$100 a month (Boost Mobile)** is all it costs for unlimited calling, texting, and data on *four* family phones. Each gets 1.5 gigabytes of high-speed data; after that, the speed slows down unless you pay for more of the high-speed stuff. (It winds up being too slow for video streaming, but fine for email and web surfing.) Handy bonus: Even if you stop paying, you can still receive incoming calls and texts for two months, free.

- **$42.50 a month (Straight Talk Wireless/Walmart)** gives you unlimited calling, texting, and Internet use (data) on a smartphone. The first 5 gigabytes each month are high speed; after you've used that, the service slows down.

- **$25 a month (Republic Wireless)** gets you unlimited calling and texting on a smartphone and 1 gigabyte of data. But it gets better: If you don't use that whole gigabyte, you actually get *refunded* for the amount you didn't use. Republic's average customer winds up paying $13.82 a month. (Republic's phones make phone calls over Wi-Fi, when it's available, instead of the cellular network, which is how they keep the plan prices so low.)

- **$19 a month (CellNuvo)** gets you 5,000 "credits" a month to use on a smartphone. You can spend these credits as any proportion of text messages (one credit each), calling minutes (10 each), or megabytes of data (10 each). If you do that stuff in a Wi-Fi hotspot, you don't use up any credits.

You can get more credits for free by watching an ad or filling out a survey.

Also: If, at the end of a month, you haven't used any credits (by sticking to Wi-Fi, for example), you're not billed the $19 for the following month.

- **$16.60 a month (TracFone),** paid as $200 a year in advance, gets you 1,500 calling minutes or text messages to use all year long—about two hours of yakking a month. (A text message costs the same as one minute of talking.)

- **$9 a month (TracFone)** gets you 30 minutes of calls (non-smartphone). As long as you keep the service, unused minutes roll over month to month. If you don't sign up for auto-renewal every month, the service is $1 more.

- **$8.33 a month (TracFone)** is the price if you pay for a whole *year* in advance ($100). It gets you 400 calling minutes or text messages to use during the year—a good safety net for the infrequent caller.

- **Free (CellNuvo).** This setup, called the Infinite plan, will take some explaining. But, yes, it's possible to have a smartphone with free service.

This company starts you out with 2,500 free "credits," which you can spend on calls, texts, or data as described already (see "$19 a month"). You can refill your credits infinitely by watching ads, taking surveys, or accepting a "thank-you" text from the company. Or, if you're impatient, you can buy 2,500 more credits for $10. Either way, you have to scrape up 2,500 new credits each month to keep your service alive.

There are also some taxes and a $25 activation fee. But overall, if you're a person with more time than money, CellNuvo is the closest thing you'll ever see to a free cell phone.

Note that these prices don't include the phone itself. Phones might cost $0 for a very simple phone, $20 for a basic Android smartphone, or $600 for a new iPhone or Samsung Galaxy. Usually, you can supply your own phone—maybe one you've snapped up used from someone on eBay or Craigslist.

So where do you buy the "gas" for your prepaid phone? You can buy a phone card for your brand in gas stations, drugstores, and so on—or you can just pay on their website. Either way, you get a code that you type or scan into the phone.

The bottom line: Prepaid phones are one of the biggest money-saving secrets left on earth.

**Savings ballpark: $1,120 a year per person**
*$1,120 = Savings off the average American cell phone bill of $110 a month by switching to TracFone's 1,500-minutes-a-month plan*

---

# Choose a different energy supplier

Here's a handy difference between your parents' era and yours: If you live in one of the enlightened states, *you* aren't stuck with one energy company. You can shop and compare utility companies as though they were cell phone carriers.

These states have deregulated electricity, gas, or both: Connecticut, Delaware, Georgia, Illinois, Indiana, Massachusetts, Maryland, Michigan, New Jersey, New York, Ohio, Pennsylvania, and Texas. (To find out what kind of deregulation your state has, click its name at saveonenergy.com/state-information.)

In these states, energy companies compete for your attention and your dollars. With a little research, you can usually find one that charges less than your current supplier. Or maybe you'll decide to switch suppliers not for price reasons, but because you prefer an energy company that gets its power from renewable sources like sunshine and wind. Either way, you can wind up with something *better* than what you have now.

What's amazing about all this is that *nothing changes on your end*. Nobody comes to the house to fiddle with the wiring. You don't start getting bills from a new company. Your current electric company still handles the wiring and the billing; the only difference is where it gets the power from.

As you undertake this very special shopping trip, you'll want answers to three questions:

- **Is the lower price just a promotional introductory rate?** If so, you risk a *higher* bill after that teaser period.

- **Does this supplier contract renew automatically every year?** It's better if they have to ask your permission each time.

- **Am I getting a fixed or floating rate?** A fixed price (per kilowatt-hour) never changes during your contract. You win if market prices go up; you lose if they go down.

If you like the sound of all this, the next step is to look over the offers of suppliers in your state. There *are* websites that compare them, but few are complete, and some are paid to promote certain suppliers.

The better road is to look over the list of suppliers on *your state's* website. Use Google to search for *ohio energy suppliers list* (or whatever your state is)—and click the web result whose address ends in ".gov" or ".us" or ".org." That's the official state list.

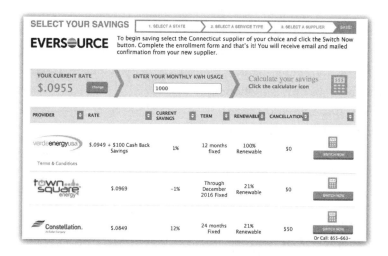

### Savings ballpark: $290 a year

*$290 = 27 percent savings from a typical 9.55-cents-per-kilowatt-hour electric utility rate, based on the average U.S. household electricity consumption of 11,000 kWh per year*

---

# How to get money for your old gadgets

When you buy an electronic device these days, it's not like you're buying a house or a grandfather clock. This isn't exactly a once-in-a-lifetime purchase.

You *know* you'll be ditching it within a couple of years, to make room for a newer, better model.

If you just toss your now-obsolete device in the trash, you're not only doing a disservice to the environment (there are toxic components in there!)—but you're also shortchanging *yourself.* Those old gadgets are worth money.

Your first stop should be one of the online gadget recycling sites, like Gazelle.com. Here even a three-year-old used phone might get you, say, $35. And the process couldn't be easier. Gazelle sends you a box with the return postage already on it. Put in the phone, send it away, and cash the check. (Gazelle accepts even broken phones.)

You should also check out ecoATM.com to see if there's an ecoATM near you. There are several thousand in the U.S.

These remarkable machines accept old phones, tablets, and music players, using clever automation to inspect the innards and outards of your device to assess its condition.

If it has any value, the machine spits out cash into your hand and slurps in your device for refurbishing or recycling. (To prevent bad guys from using ecoATMs to make money by selling stolen gadgets, it asks for your driver's license and thumbprint.)

If your gadget is so old or so broken that nobody would possibly want it, drop it off at a Best Buy or RadioShack store. Those companies offer free recycling. Just drop off your stuff and sleep well, knowing that any valuable parts of your junk will be reclaimed and reused—and that the rest will be safely disposed of.

**Earnings ballpark: $40 per gadget**
*$40 = Gazelle offer for a good-condition Samsung Galaxy S4*

------------------------------------------------------------

# The sneaky way to avoid data-overrun penalties

The cell phone carriers really have it made. They charge you for your smartphone's use of Internet data, which is measured in gigabytes consumed per month. Well, fine, except how can you possibly *predict* how much you'll need this month?

That's an impossibility. You can't even see how much you're using *now*! Quick: How many gigabytes is a web page? An email? A YouTube video?

It's not like a car, where there's a gas gauge staring you in the face. There's no meter on your phone that shows how much you're using at this moment, or how much you've used this month.

(Oh, you can look up your consumption so far on the carrier's website—somewhere. And some smartphones keep track in Settings—somewhere. But it's not prominent in either case, and very few people know about it.)

This setup is no accident. The cell phone carriers *hope* you'll go over your monthly allotment. If you do, they slap absurd overage charges onto your bill: $15 *per gigabyte*, if you use Verizon or AT&T.

That's not a rare occurrence, either. In a given three-month period, about 20 percent of all Verizon customers, and

28 percent of all AT&T customers, go over their limits and have to pay overage charges.

(If you have T-Mobile, you can ignore this entire tip. With T-Mo, if you exceed your monthly allotment, you don't incur a penalty. Instead, your Internet just slows down—it will be good for email and web surfing but too slow for video streaming. You can buy more high-speed data if you wish, but you're never cut off, and you never pay penalties.)

If you've ever been slapped with an overage charge, then do what you can never to repeat it again. Paying $15 for a gigabyte of data is like paying $250 for a glass of water.

Here are your options for tracking your data use:

- **Install a free "fuel gauge" app.** These apps, like DataMan and My Data Manager, watch your data use all day long. They warn you, with pop-up messages, as you reach certain thresholds in your monthly data—at 85 percent, 40 percent, or whatever levels you like. My Data Manager can actually do this for all the phones on a family plan, so that you, the wise adult, always have an eye on how things are going this month.

- **Adjust your cap month by month.** If, in a certain month, it looks like you or your family is going to exceed your monthly allotment of data, call the carrier and change plans—just for this month! The next more expensive plan usually costs about $15 or $20 more for the month but gets you *twice or three times* the data. In other words, instead of paying $15 for *1* gigabyte of overage penalty, you'll pay $15 and get *3 or 6* more gigabytes.

  There's nothing to stop you from "riding" your cell phone plan like this, month after month, upgrading and downgrading as necessary. (Kids going to camp for the summer without their phones? Then knock down your plan to a lower, cheaper data bucket!)

- **Identify the gas-guzzlers.** Different apps use different amounts of data, and you might be astonished to see which ones are the guilty parties. Your phone shows exactly that breakdown. On an iPhone, open Settings→Cellular, and on an Android phone, open Settings→Data Usage.

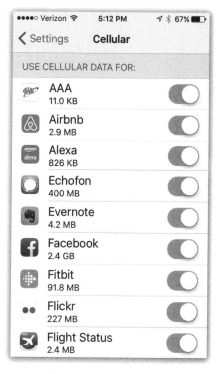

In their settings, data-hungry apps like Twitter and Facebook even offer options not to auto-play videos. That's a great idea, since videos eat up data fast.

Finally, of course, remember that whenever you're in a Wi-Fi hotspot, you're not using up any of your monthly data allowance. Go nuts—use all the data you want. Your data limit is for *cellular* data—when you're *not* in Wi-Fi.

### Savings ballpark: $60 a year

*$60 = What you'd pay if you went over your data allotment four times in a year*

# Chapter 6:
# Travel

If you ask people what they'll do if they win the lottery, "Travel the world" is usually one of the first answers. Because travel, as everybody knows, is expensive.

Fortunately, it doesn't have to be as pricey as everybody thinks.

---

## A tip about tipping overseas

In the U.S., it's customary to leave a 15 to 20 percent tip for your restaurant waiter, 10 to 15 percent for a taxi driver.

It comes as a surprise to many people, though, that those *aren't* the customs in other countries.

In some countries, the tip is automatically added to the bill. In others, a *service charge* is added to the bill, but you're supposed to leave a small tip on top of it. And in some countries, leaving a tip is actually considered an insult!

The main lesson here is this: Do some research before you go. Google *tipping in spain* or wherever you plan to go.

Here's what you might find in some sample countries:

- **Argentina.** Restaurant tips: 10 percent. Porters: 25 pesos a bag. Taxis: Round the fare up to the nearest 10 pesos.

- **Australia, New Zealand.** Restaurant tips: 10 to 15 percent. Porters: $1 a bag (that's local dollars). Taxis: Round the fare up to the nearest dollar.

- **Brazil, Chile.** Restaurant tips are built into the bill. Porters: $2 a bag. Taxis: Round the fare up to the nearest dollar.

- **Canada.** Same as in the U.S.

- **China.** This is a no-tipping culture. (If it's a hotel that caters mostly to luxury-travel foreigners, you can tip the luggage boy a little bit, but that's the only exception.)

- **Ecuador.** Restaurant tips are included in the bill. Porters: $1 a bag. Taxis: No tip is expected.

- **England, Ireland, Scotland.** Service charge is usually built into the bill; if not, add 10 percent. Bartenders don't expect tips. Porters: £1 or £2 per bag. Taxis: No tip expected, but people often round up to the nearest pound.

- **Egypt.** Restaurant tips are included in the bill, but you can add 5 or 10 percent more. Porters: $1 a bag. (Yes, U.S. dollars are preferred.) Taxis: 10 to 15 percent.

- **France.** Restaurant tips: 10 percent, unless the bill says *Service compris* ("Service included"). Porters: €2 a bag. Taxis: 10 to 15 percent.

- **Germany.** Restaurant tips: 10 to 15 percent. Porters: €2 a bag. Taxis: €1 or €2.

- **Greece.** Restaurant tips: 5 or 10 percent. Porters: €1 a bag. Taxis: None, or round up to the nearest euro.

- **India.** Restaurant tips: 10 percent, if the charge isn't already on the bill. Porters: 50 rupees a bag. Taxis: No tips expected.

- **Israel.** Restaurant tips are included in the bill, but you can add a shekel per person in your party. Porters: 6 shekels a bag. Taxis: 10 to 15 percent.

- **Italy.** Restaurant tips: included in the bill; you can round up the bill by a few euro. Porters: €1 a bag. Taxis: Tipping is not expected.

- **Japan.** This is another no-tipping culture; tips may actually be declined or considered insulting.

- **Mexico.** Restaurant tips: 10 to 15 percent. Porters: 10 or 20 pesos a bag. Taxis: No tip is expected.

- **South Africa.** Restaurant tips: Leave 10 to 15 percent. Porters: $1 a bag. Taxis: 10 percent.

- **South Pacific (Fiji, Tahiti, Samoa).** No tipping. You're considered family.

- **Switzerland.** Service charge is built into the bill; round up if you're delighted with the service. Porters: 1 or 2 francs per bag. Taxis: No tip expected.

The amounts listed here are samples, and this guide doesn't mean you *shouldn't* tip hairdressers, tour guides, and housekeepers.

In all cases (except Asia), of course, you're welcome to break these rules if you get really great service—when a concierge does you a favor, for example, or when a taxi driver helps you with luggage.

# The fallacy of travel-points credit cards

When you walk through a typical airport, two things bombard you: The miracle that a transportation system this complicated can work at all—and ads for airline credit cards.

The beauty of an airline credit card, of course, is that it gives you frequent-flier miles for every dollar you spend on anything.

The great fallacy, though, is that that's the best way to work up to free flights.

When you do the math, you discover that it's usually smarter to get a cash-back credit card like the ones described on page 46. You wind up with *cash* instead of airline points—cash that gets you closer to a free flight faster than those points would. Cash that gives you the freedom to choose any flight on any airline, to enjoy a vast selection of less expensive flights and fewer restrictions than you'd face when cashing in your frequent-flier points.

(If you're sold on the idea of a card that earns you airline miles, at least get one that rewards your spending with *universal* frequent-flier miles—points that you can convert to *any* airline's loyalty program. For example, the Chase Sapphire Preferred card earns double points when you spend on travel and restaurants, plus 20 percent off all travel booked through the card's travel site.) —*Andrea Butter*

## Savings ballpark: $90 a year
*$90 = What you'd get back from $500 monthly spending on a card that averages 3 percent cash back, minus the cash value of the points you'd earn for the same purchases, assuming a value of 1.5 cents per frequent-flier mile*

---

# How to get foreign currency without being swindled

You can't spend dollars in France, or euros in Canada. When you travel to another country, you usually have to spend money in *its currency.*

The question then becomes: What's the best way to do that, without getting bilked by greedy exchange rates and fees?

Here's how to deal with foreign currency, from worst to best.

- **Worst: Exchange it at the airport.** Those currency-exchange booths know darned well that you've just landed, you're disoriented, and you're feeling helpless without any local cash. So they'll exchange your currency, no problem—at an exchange rate that's about 10 percent worse than the actual going rate. Just for you.

- **Banks.** Don't exchange money in person at a bank, either. Here again, they're in the business of making money from poor international saps like you. If you *must* exchange money at a bank, do it in the destination country—not here at home. The rate in your home-country bank is much worse. —*Connie Lund*

| Currency | Buying Rate | Selling Rate |
|---|---|---|
| USD | 29.75 | 30.55 |
| GBP | 47.85 | 49.27 |
| EUR | 42.21 | 43.18 |
| CNY | 4.28 | 4.88 |
| JPY | 37.45 | 38.94 |
| MYR | 9.21 | 10.28 |
| AUD | 31.68 | 32.85 |
| HKD | 3.77 | 4.00 |
| KOR | 0.022 | 0.033 |
| PHP | 0.47 | 0.76 |

NICK HUBBARD/FLICKR

- **Travelers checks.** Not so great, either. Yes, you have some loss protection. But the exchange rate is poor, you have to carry them around, they're prime targets for thieves, and not all stores overseas accept them.

- **Pay with dollars.** Some foreign establishments accept payment in American cash. Often, though, that merchant will perform the conversion at a highly unfavorable rate (to you). Know the going rate ahead of time.

The other downside of carrying cash, of course, is that if you lose it or your pocket is picked, you're just hosed.

- **Withdraw money from an ATM.** If you must use local cash, use your bank ATM card to make a cash-machine withdrawal. The exchange rate will be honest, and the fee is usually very small (a percent or two). Avoid multiple *small* withdrawals, though, because each one racks up a couple of bucks in ATM-use surcharges.

And by the way: Use your bank card for this, *not your credit card or debit card*! There's a difference. If you withdraw money using a credit card, it's considered a cash advance. When you get home and get your statement, the fees and interest you've been charged will hit you in the head like a loaf of old French bread.

(A few debit cards are specially designed not to nail you with those fees, but you'd know if you had one.)

- **Buy everything possible with your credit card.** When you pay for things in other countries using your card, you get the best possible exchange rate. You don't wind up exchanging more money than you need, as you usually do with ATM withdrawals. Plus, even if your pocket is picked, it's not your financial responsibility.

The only downside is that most credit cards sock you with a 2 or 3 percent foreign transaction fee. There's a way to avoid that, though, too:

- **Best: Get yourself a "no foreign transaction fee" credit card.** On big-ticket items like hotels, restaurants, and train tickets, the usual 2 to 3 percent credit card foreign fees add up.

Some credit cards don't charge that fee, though. Capital One cards, for example, don't charge you anything extra overseas. If you're going to be abroad for more than a few days, it's well worth getting one of these cards just for this purpose.

This kind of card, in other words, is the ideal setup: great exchange rate, theft protection, *and* no fees.

One last thing: It's wise to call your credit card company before your trip. For two reasons: First, to find out what the transaction fees will be. Second, to let them know that you're traveling, so that your spending in a new country won't trigger a fraud alert and get your account shut down right when you need it most.

**Savings ballpark: $125 a week**

*$125 = $75 savings on credit card foreign-transaction fees (2.5 percent on $3,000 of spending) + 10 percent savings by avoiding scammy exchange rates on $500 of currency*

- - - - - - - - - - - - - - - - - - - - - - - - - - - - - - - - - - - - - - - - -

# How to avoid the $6,000 cell phone bill after a trip

It's one of the most outrageous pricing schemes in the modern world. When you travel abroad with your smartphone, you're subject to obscenely high *international roaming* rates—for Internet use, text messages, and phone calls. To this day, you hear about unwitting Americans returning home to bills for thousands of dollars.

You can outsmart all of this, though. Here's what you need to know:

- **Put your phone into airplane mode but turn on Wi-Fi.** Now you can get online whenever you're in a Wi-Fi hotspot, but you'll never use the cellular network, so you'll never run up any charges.

- **Call your cell phone carrier before you travel.** If you sign up for its overseas-traveler plan, you can pay a one-time monthly surcharge (it's $6 for AT&T, for example) in exchange for much lower roaming rates.

- **If you're on T-Mobile, don't worry.** Internet use and text messages are free overseas, and phone calls to other countries are 20 cents a minute. (This free service is *slow*—fine for email but not for videos. You can pay for faster speed if you need it.)

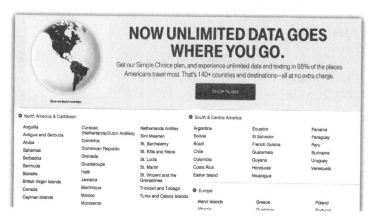

If you plan to do a lot of calling, texting, and surfing, and you'll be abroad for a while, it might even be worth renting a phone (or a SIM card) that will use local rates.

### Savings ballpark: $950 per trip

*$950 = Your cost for Verizon overseas roaming: 60 minutes of phone calls at $1.79 a minute, 60 text messages at 50 cents per text, and 400 MB of Internet use at $2.05 per megabyte*

---

# You may not need a rental car

For decades, going on vacation has, for many families, included renting a car.

In the age of UberX and Lyft, you may not need to bother.

A refresher: These are services that let you summon a car and driver on demand, just by tapping a button on your smartphone. Lyft and UberX both employ ordinary folks (fully background-checked) in their own family cars, at a huge savings to you. Much cheaper than a taxi. (UberX is much less expensive than Uber's better-known service, Uber Black, which summons a commercial car service.)

 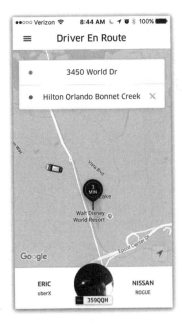

Depending on how much driving you plan to do, it may be *far* more cost-effective to summon UberX or Lyft whenever you need to move from place to place. You save not only on the cost of the rental, but also the cost of parking, both at your hotel every night and at the theme park (or wherever you're going).

Let's say you're going to Orlando for a week of theme-park fun. Car rentals are about $45 a day. Parking at Disney World or Universal Studios is $20 a day. Parking at your hotel might be $10 a night. So for the luxury of having your own car, you're looking at $525 for the week.

A typical 10-mile UberX or Lyft ride, on the other hand, costs about $10. So for the week of getting to and from the theme parks (and to and from the airports), you'll pay about $160.

As a bonus, the car is already air-conditioned when you climb in, and you never have to look for parking. You're always dropped off right at the door, which may save you a scorching 15-minute trudge across a theme-park parking lot at the beginning and end of every day.

Of course, Lyft and UberX are ideal for getting somewhere specific, not for serendipitous exploring. But on many vacations (and *most* business trips), renting a car and driver for each trip makes far more sense than renting and driving your own car for the whole week.

### Savings ballpark: $365 per trip
$365 = Savings by taking 16 UberX trips at $10 each, vs. renting a car for a weekly $525

------------------------------------------------------------

# Never pay full price for Disney tickets—or wait in Disney lines

A h, Disney World! (Or ah, Disneyland!)

For many lucky children, a Disney vacation is an iconic part of youth. They'll always remember that joyous, carefree trip—primarily because they didn't realize how much their parents paid for tickets, and they've forgotten the hours they stood in line.

Truth is, there are ways to address both problems.

- **Understand the tickets.** There are so many different kinds of Disney World tickets! At least 54 of them, actually. So telling you to "understand the tickets" is a little like suggesting that you "understand neuroscience." But here goes.

*Magic Your Way tickets* are the base-model tickets, good for entering one Disney Orlando theme park each day (Magic Kingdom, Epcot, Hollywood Studios, Animal Kingdom).

You can buy them for any number of days from one to 10; the more days, the lower the price per day. A one-day ticket might be $132; a five-dayer works out to about $72 a day. (For one-day tickets, the price varies by demand. It's most expensive during school vacations and holidays, for example.)

*Park Hopper* is a feature you can *add* to a base ticket for $40 to $70, depending on how many days your base ticket goes. It gives you permission to go to *more than one* major park in a single day. (Usually, the Park Hopper isn't worth it for Disney World; you can easily spend a full day at each park. It's a better deal at Disney*land,* in California, because the two parks—Disneyland and Disney California Adventure—are adjacent. It's more practical to park hop.)

The *Water Park Fun & More* add-on gets you into Disney's two Orlando water parks, two mini-golf courses, and one regular golf course. It adds about $68 to the price of the base ticket.

- **Buy tickets online.** You'll pay the *most* if you buy your tickets in person, at the park.

  Instead, buy them from authorized ticket sites, like OfficialTicketCenter.com, UndercoverTourist.com, and ParkSavers.com. They sell almost every kind of Disney ticket at a discount. A standard five-day Magic Your Way pass, for example, might go for $327. That's $13 off Disney's own online price, and $35 off the price at the gate.

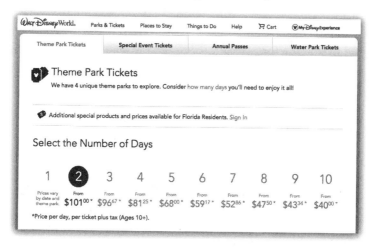

(Caution: *Fake* Disney passes are a thriving scam online—on eBay, Craigslist, and unauthorized websites. Don't fall for it. Disney tickets are linked to the owner's fingerprint, so if you buy these tickets online, you won't be able to use them at the park.)

- **Buy tickets in advance.** Here's a sweet trick: Disney theme-park prices go up once or twice every year. But a multiday ticket never expires. So if you're sure you're going to visit a Disney park *someday,* buying sooner saves you money over buying later.

(Exceptions: A *one*-day ticket expires at the end of the following year. So if you buy a ticket in March 2017, it expires at the end of 2018. And a multiday ticket has to be used within 14 days of the *first* time you use it.)

- **Reserve your FastPass+ rides now.** FastPass+ is an online ride-reservation system. (It replaces the old paper-based FastPass system.) Using the My Disney Experience phone app or website, you can actually reserve a spot on a certain Disney ride for a certain time—and when you show up, you skip the line! You've just saved yourself an hour or *two* per ride!

Of course, if *everybody* could do this, it wouldn't work. So the *number* of FastPass+ spots is limited—and they book up, sometimes weeks in advance.

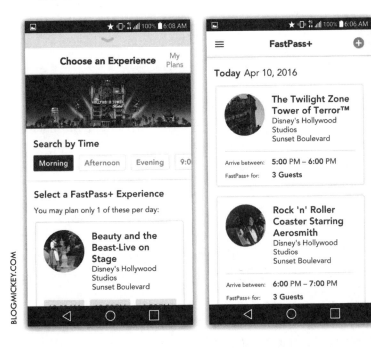

That's why you should buy your Disney park ticket online and then *reserve your FastPass+ time slots* as soon as possible. This trick is *hugely* important to a successful Disney park visit.

(You can make up to three bookings in advance. After you've used them up, you can make additional FastPass+ appointments using kiosks in the park, although open slots are subject to availability.)

Do some research online (at DisneyTouristBlog.com, for example) to see which rides are worth booking first.

### Savings ballpark: $140 per family, and eight hours of standing in lines
*$140 = Savings on a five-day Magic Your Way pass for a family of four, bought online vs. buying at the gate*

- - - - - - - - - - - - - - - - - - - - - - - - - - - - - - - - - - - - - - - - - - -

# The Gogo in-flight refund

As though it's not enough of a miracle that you can sit in a chair and fly through the sky, now you can do it while *surfing the Internet*. Most planes these days are equipped with in-flight Wi-Fi—usually for a hefty price.

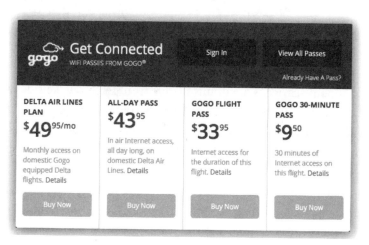

Behind the scenes—well, actually, above or below the scenes—the Internet signal is coming either from satellites or from ground stations. These systems are massively expensive to set up (hence the high price of the service).

They're also frequently so slow that they're unusable.

Of course, you don't discover that until *after* you've paid for Wi-Fi for your whole flight (or for the month or year). That's why, if you discover that you can't get anything done online, you should absolutely, positively report the problems once you land.

The representatives of Gogo and the other in-flight Wi-Fi services hear about such unusable Wi-Fi flights all day long, and they have your back. They immediately refund what you paid or otherwise make you whole.

Just don't forget.

### Savings ballpark: $34 per flight
*$34 = Refunded price of a one-day Gogo pass*

- - - - - - - - - - - - - - - - - - - - - - - - - - - - - - - - - - - - - -

# The ol' hotel-restaurant takeout trick

Room service is a glorious luxury. You perch on the side of your hotel-room bed, pick up the phone, and order anything you want. Thirty minutes later, there's a magical knock on the door. It's a nattily dressed worker, bearing your food on a tray.

But room service is known as a luxury for a reason. By the time you've factored in the inflated room-service prices, *and* the service/delivery charge, *and* the gratuity, you've paid double or triple what the food is worth.

Ah, but there's another way to enjoy hotel-restaurant food while slumped on your hotel-room bed watching TV: Go downstairs and get the food *yourself.*

Make your way to the hotel's restaurant and tell the host or hostess that you'd like to order something to take back to your room. Place your order and wait for it there, much the way you'd wait for any takeout food.

Boom: No inflated prices, no service charge, no tip. Just the same delicious hot food, carried back to your room by *you.*

If you're feeling guilty, tip yourself.

### Savings ballpark: $15 per meal
$15 = Savings on a club sandwich + beverage when picked up from a restaurant ($15) instead of room service ($30)

---

# European travel advisory: Get the VAT you've got coming to you

Sales tax is a fact of life, right? After all, *someone's* got to fund the government so that it can maintain its schools, roads, and police force.

In Europe, they don't call it sales tax. Without a hint of irony, they call it the value added tax, or VAT. And it's a whopper: It's a *20 to 25 percent* tax on most goods and services. (The rate depends on the country. It's 20 percent in England, 23 percent in Ireland, 25 percent in Scandinavia, and so on.)

Somewhere along the line, it occurred to an American traveler in Europe: "Excuse me, but why am *I* paying sales tax here? I don't live here. I won't benefit from those roads and schools! I shouldn't have to pay that tax!"

And so today, indeed, you can get *back* all the sales tax you've paid during a European vacation. (You get back the VAT on *things* you've bought, not *services* like hotels and meals. Unless you're a business traveler.)

Now, be warned: This book's promise is not to offer time-for-money swaps—not to make you *work* for money—and this tip *barely* qualifies. Getting your VAT refund is not quick and easy. They've made it so complex and time-consuming that most people never make the effort, which is why travelers leave hundreds of millions of dollars behind every year.

But if you've done a fair amount of shopping on your trip, the hassle might be worth it. The steps vary by country, but in general, it goes like this:

- **When you're shopping.** Shop at stores that participate in the VAT-refund thing. Major stores, and stores in tourist cities, do. Often, there's a sign in the window. If not, ask.

  To get the VAT refund, you have to spend enough at each shop to reach the country's minimum, which varies. (In Ireland, it's €30, which is around $33. In England, it's £30—or about $43. In Italy, it's €155—roughly $172. Google it before you go.)

  *As you pay for your stuff,* ask for the VAT refund form, which the salesperson has to fill out. You'll probably be asked to show your passport. If you don't get this form at the time of purchase, you'll never get the refund.

*Keep your receipt.* In fact, attach it to the form. Without all this paperwork, you won't get your refund.

• **As you leave the country.** You'll turn in all this paperwork at your *last stop* in the European Union, even if you've visited a few countries. (If you're not in the European Union—Switzerland or Norway, say—do this wrapping-up process as you leave those countries.)

At the airport, train station, seaport, or border crossing, *before* you check in for your flight, train, or ship, visit the Customs desk or office. (Leave time for this; you'll probably have to hunt to find Customs and stand in line.) Present your forms and receipts. The Customs agent may even ask to *see* the stuff you bought, to make sure you're not cheating. That's an argument for visiting Customs before you check your bags.

The Customs officer stamps your forms.

Now all you have to do is convert those forms to *money*—your refund.

Many stores work with refund services called things like Premiere Tax Free or Global Blue, whose offices are somewhere there in the airport. The handy part here is that they give you your refund on the spot, in cash (in exchange for a 4 percent fee), or else as a credit on your credit card.

Otherwise, you have to mail the stamped forms. Sometimes, there are postage-free envelopes, already addressed, right there at the airport. If not, mail them once you get home. (And don't forget. There's a time limit on all of this, usually 30 or 60 days.)

The refund may arrive as a credit on your card within a few months, or as a check in the mail.

If you're visiting Australia, it's the goods and services tax (GST, 9 percent) and wine equalisation tax (WET, 14.5 percent). The minimum purchase per store is $300 Australian (about $224 in U.S. currency). You get your refund at the airport or seaport, as described above.

In Japan, it's called the consumption tax (8 percent, rising to 10 percent in 2017). No fussing at the airport required: The tax is taken right off the charge when you buy the stuff or, worst case, you have to take your receipt to a tax-refund desk right there in the store.

### Savings ballpark: $200 per vacation
*$200 = 20 percent VAT refunds on $1,000*
*worth of purchases during your trip*

# Duty free:
# A jargon-free explanation

O K. Now that you understand the concept of the VAT (as described in the previous tip), suddenly the concept of the duty-free shop will make sense.

ALEXANDER PODSHIVALOV, DREAMSTIME

When you're passing through an airport or seaport, you could argue that you're not really *in* a country. So duty-free shops are stores where they *don't* add on those whopping sales taxes, like VAT, GST, or consumption tax.

On top of that, they don't pass on the *import* taxes that are normally built into the prices of imported products like liquor, tobacco, perfume, and jewelry. (Which is why duty-free shops tend to be mostly stocked with liquor, tobacco, perfume, and jewelry.)

Sounds great, right? You can buy stuff without being charged that massive 20 or 33 percent tax, and without having to go through the ritual of trying to get it back! In theory, that should save you a ton on things that are traditionally taxed to the hilt.

In practice, duty-free shops aren't really much of a deal. Many of them now *mark up* their goods by that 20 or 33 percent. So you don't save anything, but they pocket the equivalent of the taxes.

You *may* get discounts on tobacco; you *can* get deals on alcohol. Perfume and jewelry are usually less expensive outside the airport, though, once you get your VAT refund.

And souvenir-type stuff is *always* less expensive outside the airport.

The bottom line: Don't buy anything at a duty-free shop unless you already know how much it would have cost downtown and you're convinced that it's a deal.

**Scam ballpark: 25 percent markup**

-------------------------------------------------------------

# The beauty of an Airbnb trip

Airbnb.com is one of the great Internet-economy success stories. It's a website where you can sign up to stay in *someone's home,* instead of a hotel, when you travel.

Staying in an Airbnb offers three enormous benefits when you travel, and only two of them have to do with money.

First, Airbnbs are usually much cheaper than hotels. Second, because it's a house or apartment, you can buy some groceries and make your own meals instead of eating in restaurants—further savings.

Finally, and maybe most importantly, an Airbnb is not a hotel. The rooms aren't cookie-cutter clones, boring and commercial. You're staying someplace that feels like a *home*; by the

time you leave, you feel like you've really *lived* in your destination city, instead of just toured it.

Usually, the house or apartment is all yours; the owner isn't there. (Either they're away, or it's a house they maintain exclusively for renting out.) Occasionally, they're also home, but you get your own bedroom or your own part of the house; these setups, of course, are *really* inexpensive.

To book an Airbnb, you visit Airbnb.com, type in your destination, and scroll through the photos and descriptions of homes available. You can read reviews left by people who've stayed there before you, ask questions, and look over photo portfolios.

If you find one that looks good, enter the dates you want to claim; within 24 hours, the owner emails you back to let you know if those dates are free.

Savvy travelers have come to think of Airbnb this way: much more interesting lodging for much less money.

### Savings ballpark: $210 a night

*$210 = Savings by renting a New York City "cozy Wall Street room" apartment for one night ($80) vs. a night at the New York Marriott Downtown ($290)*

# Earn frequent-flier miles with hotel stays

A few hotels offer frequent-flier miles for certain airlines. No secret there.

But sites like PointsHound.com and RocketMiles.com go much further. These are hotel-booking sites, just like Hotels.com or whatever—but each booking earns you a ton of airline frequent-flier points. Getting 3,000 to 6,000 "miles" per booking isn't unusual.

You choose which airline program you want to get your points, but not all airlines are available. Your choices on Points-Hound, for example, are American, Virgin, JetBlue, Alaska, and a bunch of international airlines. RocketMiles also offers United and Southwest.

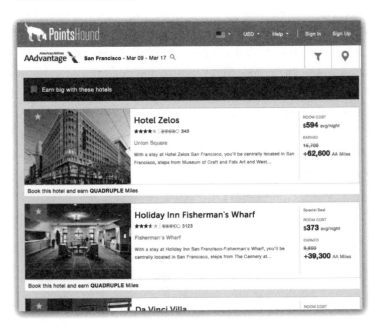

There are some footnotes. For example, you don't get *hotel* points when you book this way. Not every hotel participates, and not every price is the best you could find online (although PointsHound promises to refund the difference if you find a lower price).

Otherwise, these sites offer a clever way to reach free flights faster.

**Earnings ballpark: 5,000 miles per two-day stay**

--------------------------------------------------------------

# How to rack up frequent-flier miles without flying

The most common way to earn frequent-flier points is, of course, to fly frequently. Each airline awards points for each ticket you buy, and when you accumulate enough of them, you can trade them in for free flights. (A free round-trip domestic flight usually costs 25,000 or 50,000 miles, depending on the route, class of service, and time of year.) These programs are designed to keep you loyal to the airline.

But there are lots of other ways to accumulate and use frequent-flier points—none of which involve any flying. Some people get deeply immersed in playing the points game, hanging out online and sharing their tips (for example, FlyerTalk.com and ThePointsGuy.com). But here, to save you the time, are some points tips from Brian Kelly, the guy behind ThePointsGuy.com:

- **Airline shopping portals.** Each major airline offers a website that links to more than 850 online stores: Home Depot, Macy's, Nike, Nordstrom, Walmart, and so on. You type in the product (or store) you're looking for. If you then wind up buying something, you get two frequent-flier miles per dollar you spend. Periodic specials goose that number higher (for example, six points per dollar, or 2,500 bonus points).

Some of these shopping sites: United MileagePlus Shopping (MileagePlusShopping.com), American Airlines AAdvantage eShopping (AAdvantageeShopping.com), Southwest Rapid Rewards Shopping (RapidRewardsShopping.Southwest.com), British Airways Gate 365 (BritishAirways.com/travel/eshop), and Delta SkyMiles Shopping (SkyMilesShopping.com).

- **Bank-account sign-ups.** Banks and brokerages have always offered special rewards for opening an account. These days, though, it's not a free toaster. It's usually cash, or points for a gift program—or frequent-flier points. A *lot* of them.

A typical Citibank or Fidelity new-account reward might be 50,000 points, which is generally enough for two free airline flights. To find out when such offers come along, pay attention to the frequent-flier discussion sites mentioned above.

- **Eat at restaurants.** Most major airlines have little-known free programs that reward you with miles in exchange for eating out; see the next tip.

There are also, of course, credit cards that reward you with airline miles for every dollar you spend. As noted on page 126, just getting *cash* for using your credit card is usually a better deal—unless you fly a lot, and mostly on a single airline.

### Earnings ballpark: $780

$780 = Cash equivalent of miles (at 1.5 cents a mile), based on opening a bank account (50,000 miles) and buying $1,000 worth of goods from airline portals (2,000 miles)

-------------------------------------------------------------

# Eat your way to free flights

You've probably never heard of your favorite airline's "eat your way to free flights" program. But that's a shame, because if you eat at restaurants a few times a year, you can rack up points quickly—and this technique doesn't require you to pay anything, sign up for any card, or adopt any new habits.

Not only do you get, for example, five or eight points for every dollar you spend, but you also get a handsome sign-up bonus of 3,000 points or so.

Some 11,000 restaurants participate, which is a huge number—but your favorite may not be on the list. (The restaurant list seems to be the same for every airline since, behind the scenes, all the airlines' programs are run by the same company.)

Each program has various membership levels, determined by how often you eat out; the top tier usually requires you to eat out 12 times a year and agree to get the program's promotional emails. Here are the details, using that top tier as an example:

- **American Airlines AAdvantage Dining.** Get 1,000 frequent-flier miles for signing up, and then five miles per dollar spent. AA.rewardsnetwork.com

- **Delta SkyMiles Dining.** 3,000 miles for signing up—or 5,000 points if you're a member of Delta's frequent-flier program already. Then get five miles for every dollar you spend at the restaurants. SkyMiles.rewardsnetwork.com

- **United MileagePlus Dining.** 500-mile bonus for signing up, and 500-mile bonus each of the first five times you dine out (3,000 total). Then five miles for every dollar you spend dining out. MPDining.rewardsnetwork.com

- **Alaska Airlines Mileage Plan Dining.** 1,000-mile sign-up bonus, then five points per dollar you spend. MileagePlan.rewardsnetwork.com

- **JetBlue TrueBlue Dining.** No sign-up bonus. One point per dollar spent, or two points if you have Mosaic status (15,000 miles a year) on JetBlue's frequent-flier program. TrueBlueDining.com

- **Southwest Rapid Rewards Dining.** 750 miles for signing up. Then you get three points per dollar you spend at the restaurants, plus an extra 10 points if you submit a review of the restaurant. As an incentive to keep at it, you get 500 more miles when you've reached 1,500 dining-out points, and a 300-mile bonus every time you earn 1,000 more points by eating out. RapidRewardsDining.com

- **Hilton Hotels HHonors Dining Rewards.** Yes, a couple of hotel chains offer "frequent-flier" points for eating out, too. Earn enough of them, and you can get a free night of lodging.

  Hilton gives you 1,000 points the first time you eat out, and then 500 more each of the next two times. After that, you get eight HHonors points per dollar you spend at participating restaurants. HHonorsDining.com

- **IHG Rewards Club Dining.** The IHG (InterContinental Hotels Group) includes Holiday Inn, Kimpton, Crowne Plaza, Intercontinental, and a few smaller chains. You get 1,000 points for this hotel chain's program the first time you eat out. Then it's eight points per dollar spent. IHG.com/hotels/gb/en/diningrewards/home

Since it takes 25,000 miles to buy a free plane ticket, you might wonder if it's worth signing up for these programs. After all, you'd have to eat out 100 times (at $50 a meal) to get one free flight.

But points come from all kinds of sources: eating out, flying, staying in hotels, using credit cards, opening financial accounts. Every little source helps—and since this one costs you nothing, why not?

Now, knowing that you're eating your way to a free flight or free hotel stay is designed as an incentive to get people to eat out more. The real winners, of course, are people who *already* eat out and can now parlay that habit into extra travel goodies.

No, wait. The *real* real winners are people with credit cards that *already* give frequent-flier points for eating out, like the Chase Sapphire Preferred or American Express Rewards Gold cards (two points per dollar spent at restaurants). If you use that kind of card, you're double dipping. You get two points per dollar from the credit card, and then five or eight points from the airline's program. Spend $50 on dinner out, and you've just landed yourself 500 frequent-flier points. —*Brian Kelly, ThePointsGuy.com*

### Earnings ballpark: $120 the first year
$120 = Cash value of points earned by dining out 20 times ($50 per meal, five points per dollar) + 3,000-mile sign-up bonus

- - - - - - - - - - - - - - - - - - - - - - - - - - - - - - - - - - - - - - - -

# Fly and drive your way to free hotel rooms

As you now know, it's possible to earn free flights by staying at certain hotels. Not to turn your brain in knots, but it's also possible to do the reverse: Earn free hotel nights by booking flights!

The Starwood hotel group (Sheraton, Westin, W, and St. Regis hotels) has created reciprocal point-earning programs with Delta, Emirates Airlines, and, of all things, Uber (page 131).

You can read all the details online (starwoodhotels.com/preferredguest/account/benefits/delta/index.html), but here's the gist of it: If you're a Gold or Platinum Starwood member, and you buy a Delta or Emirates flight, you get points toward Starwood *hotel* stays (one point per dollar spent on the flight). You also get express check-in lanes for both your flights *and* your hotel stays. And you get free Wi-Fi in the hotel room, and a free checked suitcase on the flight.

You also get points the other way: Staying at Starwood hotels gets you extra frequent-flier points on Delta (at one mile per dollar).

And when you use Uber to get around, you get a Starwood point for every $1 you spend on those rides. If you use Uber to get around *while* you're staying in a Starwood hotel, it's even better: two, three, or four points per dollar, depending on your Starwood membership level.

You sign up for this free program at SPG.com/uber. (To keep your membership alive, you have to stay at least one night in one Starwood hotel a year.) —*Brian Kelly, ThePointsGuy.com*

### Earnings ballpark: $60 a year

*$60 = Cash value of 750 Delta miles earned with three hotel nights in a year (at 1.5 cents a mile) + 800 hotel points earned with three flights (value: about 5 cents per point) + 500 hotel points earned from 50 Uber rides in a year*

- - - - - - - - - - - - - - - - - - - - - - - - - - - - - - - - - - - - - - - - - -

# Cheaper flights through multiple-airline bookings

Grizzled veteran fliers sometimes murmur about the days when they'd snag amazing *hidden-city* fares. That's when you want to fly from Miami to Houston, for example. To save money, you book a flight from Miami to LA that has a *layover* in Houston—yes, that's a cheaper ticket overall—and you *get off the plane* in Houston and stay there.

Sites like SkipLagged.com can find hidden-city fares for you, but the whole thing is tricky. Airlines forbid the practice and may actually ban you from future flights if they catch you. (And, of course, this tactic works only on one-way trips.)

Tripcombi.com, though, can find discounts of up to 80 percent by using a different and perfectly legal tactic: It combines unconnected flights from rival airlines through a mutual layover airport.

Suppose you're trying to fly from New York to Berlin. You could buy a nonstop on Air Berlin for $725.

But you could also fly to London on Finnair and switch there to a British Airways flight to Berlin—for $526. You've just saved 27 percent.

In many cases, Tripcombi proposes exhaustingly inconvenient itineraries in exchange for gigantic savings, like two stops or very long travel times. But especially when you're booking international flights, which often require a layover anyway, it's worth making *one* stop—at Tripcombi.com.

**Savings ballpark: $400 per trip**
*$400 = Savings by flying from NYC to Berlin with a hidden stop in London, and a similar return flight*

------------------------------------------------------------

# Discounted cruise-ship bookings: The basics

Cruise-ship prices are like hotel-room prices. They rise and fall according to the seasons, weather, oil prices, and alignment of the planets. The sample prices listed in the brochure are much higher than what you'll actually pay, unless it's a crazy-popular, sold-out sailing. Here's how to play the cruise-fare game:

- **Reserve at the right time.** If you book your cruise (and make a deposit) at least six months before the sailing, you'll get the lowest fares—25 to 50 percent off. You'll also get first pick of cabins, and sometimes goodies like discounted airfare, free excursions, drink packages, or upgraded cabins. Booking early also means that you can make your plane and hotel reservations early, too, and save money on *those*.

- **Watch for sales.** You can find great sales on sails during certain times of year, like Wave Season. (That's what the cruise lines call January and February, when the masses book their cruises for later that year.) The other season for big sales is October, when cruise lines try to unload the holiday-season cabins that haven't yet sold.

Royal Caribbean and Celebrity offer one-day sales every week.

The best way to find out about sales is to visit Cruise Critic's Deals page (CruiseCritic.com/bargains)—or sign up for its newsletter (at CruiseCritic.com/newsletter).

- **Reserve at the last minute.** Fares generally rise steadily as the cruise approaches. Then, with a couple of months to go, you may find some spectacular (but nonrefundable) deals on cabins, reflecting the cruise line's panic that some rooms remain unbooked. The rooms may not have balconies, or they may be interior (no-window) cabins—but how much daylight time will you be spending in your cabin anyway?

- **Sail at the right time.** As with anything else in this world, supply and demand affect pricing. If you can sail during an off-peak time of year, you pay less.

  The *shoulder* periods, for example, are the weeks just before and after the most popular times. Everyone wants to go to Alaska in the summer, so there are great deals on May sailings. Everyone thinks about Bermuda for the summer or winter holidays, so the shoulder months are April and October.

  There's really no off-season in the Caribbean. But there are slower times for cruise ships: whenever the kids are in school, for example. Fares are also lower during the peak hurricane season (mid-September to mid-October).

  That's right, hurricane season. Storms hardly ever interrupt cruises, but a lot of people avoid those periods just in case— to your financial benefit.

- **Book the spa and restaurants ahead.** On big cruise ships, some cafeterias and restaurants are included in your fare. But there are also specialty, extra-cost restaurants. If you book your reservations there before the cruise, you'll pay less than if you reserve them *on* the ship. The same goes for spa treatments. (The spa is usually discounted on days when the ship is in port, too.)

- **Ask for special discounts.** You usually get 5 or 10 percent off your fare if you're 55 or older, if you're a member of AARP (page 205) or the military, or if you're a repeat cruiser—but *only if you ask* when you make the booking.

- **Book the next one on the ship.** On each cruise, you have the opportunity to book *another* cruise at a discount. In general, the deposit you put down is refundable, and the cruise you book is changeable, so you don't lose anything by exploiting this option.

Unless you hate cruising.

### Savings ballpark: $900
*$900 = Savings on a three-night Royal Caribbean cruise from Port Canaveral to the Caribbean (vs. the $1,160 brochure price) by booking an August cruise in March*

---

# The charms of the repositioning cruise

A particular ship usually makes the same run over and over: back and forth between New York and Bermuda, say.

But cruise lines sometimes rejigger their offerings. After the summer runs from New England, for example, they might move a ship to do a Mexico route for the winter. Or they might decide to move a certain ship from Miami to Europe for good, where it will make a *different* run over and over.

To get the ship over there, they have to *sail* it—and that one-time-only "repositioning run" usually comes with super-cheap fares. Since these cruises entail more days at sea (and fewer stops), they often have special themes. It might be theater, for example, or science, complete with speakers and experts.

To find these cruises, visit RepositioningCruise.com. Or ask a travel agent, call the cruise line, or search Google for, say, *carnival repositioning cruises.*

| Sailing Date | Departs From | Ends In | Cruise Line / Ship | Brochure Starting Price* | Our Starting Price | YOU SAVE!! | Status |
|---|---|---|---|---|---|---|---|
| | | | **REPOSITIONING** | | | | |
| May 27 | Colon, Panama | Lisbon, Portugal | Pullmantur / Monarch | $1,195 | $159 | 87% | 87% Off! |
| May 28 | Cartagena, Colombia | Lisbon, Portugal | Pullmantur / Monarch | - | $245 | Info | Reduced Again! |
| May 28 | Fort Lauderdale, FL | London (Dover), England | Princess / Pacific Princess | - | $1,799 | Info | Sold Out! |
| May 28 | Fort Lauderdale, FL | London (Dover), England | Princess / Pacific Princess | - | $6,759 | Info | Onboard Credit! |
| May 31 | New York (Manhattan), NY | London (Dover), England | Princess / Pacific Princess | - | $4,599 | Info | Suite! |
| Aug 24 | London (Southampton), England | New York (Brooklyn), NY | Princess / Caribbean Princess | $5,899 | $3,499 | 41% | Reduced Again! |
| Aug 28 | Copenhagen, Denmark | Boston, MA | Royal Caribbean / Serenade of the Seas | $3,209 | $1,249 | 61% | Exclusive Offer! |
| Aug 30 | Copenhagen, Denmark | New York (Brooklyn), NY | Princess / Regal Princess | - | $3,309 | Info | Onboard Credit! |

Before you book, though, do the math on the savings: These are one-way sailings. You'll have to fly yourself back again.

## Savings ballpark: $965

*$965 = Savings on a 15-night repositioning cruise from Fort Lauderdale to Rome, vs. the $2,242 brochure price*

---

# Cruise ships: Save money on board

There are clever ways to save money once you're *on* a cruise ship, too:

- **Order the bottle.** Everyone knows that ordering wine by the glass costs a lot more than wine by the bottle. But what if you can't finish the bottle at the meal? This isn't a restaurant, where they'll just pour the rest down the drain; it's a ship, and you'll be back in the same eatery another day! Your waiter will gladly save the rest of the bottle for your return.

- **Bring your own soda.** Water and iced tea are free on the ship, but you have to pay extra for any other kind of drink. If you or your kids insist on soda or juice, most cruise lines don't mind your bringing a couple of six-packs with you in your luggage. (The exception: Royal Caribbean does mind.)

  (The policy for bringing your own *alcohol* on board varies widely. Usually, it's OK to bring a bottle of wine for drinking in your cabin on departure day, but most other carry-on booze is forbidden.)

- **Eat up.** Remember, you've paid for *unlimited food.* No wonder the average cruise passenger gains seven pounds in seven days on board!

  It's probably obvious that you can eat all you want at the cafeteria-style restaurants. But it's *not* obvious that you can order all you want in the *main* dining room, too. Order two entrees. Order three desserts. Ask for a half-sized entree portion. It's all included, and it's all fine!

  You're welcome to carry food and drinks around the ship, too (to your room, for example)—even from the bars.

- **Free room service.** On most cruise lines, room service is free. Sure, tip the delivery person. But don't fear sticker shock from in-room dining, as you might in a hotel.

- **Free anti-seasickness treatments.** Seasickness medicine is generally free from the purser's desk. Or call room service and ask for crackers and green apples, which are excellent queasiness cures.

- **Don't double tip.** It's customary to tip your room attendant $10 a day, which is nice. (You wouldn't *believe* how little they're paid, and what long hours they work.) There's also a place to write in a tip for orders at the bar.

Usually, though, the cruise line adds both of these gratuities to your bill automatically. Find out before you leave your own tip.

### Savings ballpark: $125

$125 = Savings on a bottle of wine vs. individual glasses for three nights ($40) + 12 sodas or juices bought on board ($35) + accidental tips ($50)

------------------------------------------------------------

# The big secret about cruise-ship excursions

When you take a cruise, you don't just sit on a ship the whole time. Every couple of days, the ship *stops* somewhere. It spends a day at each port of call, so you can go ashore to visit a new country.

And what, exactly, will you *do* in that magical new land? Most people sign up for one of the cruise line's *excursions*: preplanned day trips.

The cruise line gives you a catalog of options for each port. You might see options for snorkeling for $80, a bus tour to the local ruins for $90, or maybe a horseback ride through the forest for $120. (If you decide to book them, you should read reviews written by people who've been on them. You can find the reviews at sites like CruiseCritic.com, AvidCruiser.com, and CruiseReviews.com.)

To run these excursions, the cruise lines hire local guides and tour companies. What very few people realize, though, is

**CRUISE CRITIC**  REVIEWS    FIND A CRUISE    DEALS

## Grand Turk Island Tour Excursion Reviews

**Overall Rating** ◉◉◉◉○

An island tour is one of the most efficient ways to learn about the historical heartbeat of Grand Turk -- the capital island of Turks and Caicos.

Tracey/Thom
4 reviews

◉◉◉◉○    May 2016

Short 2 hour tour in a mini van. Nice way to see the whole island, salt mines, wild donkeys etc.

**Read Tracey/Thom's full Carnival Splendor cruise review**

Provider: **Carnival Cruise Line**

MEMBER
jollybecute
1 review

◉◉○○○    Jun 2015

It was very bad. The food was very bad and very salty. The place where we stop for a taste of the island cuisine was dirty, the toilet has no running water to wash your hands and no water to plush. Not acceptable!

Clawman    ◉◉◉◉◉    Apr 2016

that you can hire *exactly the same* guides and companies directly yourself!

It's perfectly legal; the cruise line offers its excursions only as a courtesy.

This technique saves a lot of money. Furthermore, the group will be *you.* It'll be just your family, or just you and your companions: a far more personalized and memorable adventure.

For best results, line up your guides before the cruise. You can take care of everything by email. To find good tours, Google what you want (use the cruise line's options as a starting point, if you like): *cancun snorkel tours* or *santorini walking tour guide.*

You'll find the tour operators' websites full of prices and options. Check reviews from previous travelers.

In theory, booking the excursion through the cruise line does offer one unmistakable benefit: If you're late getting back, they guarantee that the ship won't sail without you. Or, if it does, the cruise line will pay your way to meet the ship at the next port.

In practice, though, that situation is almost unheard of; any guide you hire is perfectly capable of getting you back to the ship by the deadline.

### Savings ballpark: $360 per cruise
*$360 = Savings of 30 percent off three cruise-line excursions, $100 per person, for a family of four*

--------------------------------------------------------

# Resell a hotel room you can't use

S tuck with a hotel-room reservation you can't use—and can't cancel? List it on hotel-room reselling sites RoomerTravel.com or Cancelon.com; you can name your price.

Those sites then list rooms on travel-search sites like Kayak and Trivago, in the hopes that fellow travelers will stumble across them. If someone buys your room (there's no guarantee), Roomer and Cancelon take a 10 or 15 percent cut.

You may not break even, but you won't have wasted $300, either.

### Savings ballpark: $225
*$225 = Typical amount you'll get back after successfully listing a room for $250 (minus the RoomerTravel fee)*

# Chapter 7:
# Cars

There's an old joke that goes, "What's the definition of a boat? A hole in the water into which you pour money."

In that case, a car is a *wheeled platform* into which you pour money.

The purchase price is only the beginning. Then there's the gas, insurance, maintenance, tires, taxes, licensing, registration, finance charges, and depreciation (you know, that thing that makes a new car's value drop by half the instant you drive it off the lot).

Trying to plug the cash leaks of your car is well worth the effort, as you're about to find out.

----------------------------------------

## The cheapest gas right now

Apps—those millions of little smartphone programs—have already revolutionized shopping online, booking flights, and dating. Why shouldn't they also put the power of gas prices in your hand?

The app is GasBuddy, and it's free. It's available in iPhone and Android versions. Open it up, and it shows the current gas prices at all gas stations near you (or at any location you specify). That's it!

And how can one app somehow know the prices, *at this moment*, from every gas station on earth? Easy: It's crowdsourced. Your fellow citizens report the prices every time they stop at a gas station.

To encourage participation, Gas Buddy offers them points and a chance to win $100 in gas every day. If you want to help your fellow drivers, by all means participate by reporting prices. In the meantime, you may as well exploit their mass wisdom by driving an extra three minutes to save 15 cents a gallon.

### Savings ballpark: $80 a year

*$80 = Savings of 15 cents a gallon for a 25 mpg car driven the average American's 13,200 miles a year, with gas at $3 per gallon*

# Fuel-conscious driving: The basics

The best way to save money on gas is to buy a fuel-efficient car in the first place—or an electric one.

But science has shown that there are plenty of ways to increase your mileage no matter what car you're driving. Here it is: the assembled wisdom of the car-driving ages.

- **Coast to a stop.** Braking converts your car's momentum, which you've burned gas to achieve, into wasted heat from friction. So if you *know* you're going to be stopping—because you can see a stop sign or a light that's red or yellow—take your foot off the gas as early as you can! Use less gas, brake less, and coast to stops as often as possible.

  Learning to scan ahead for your next stop, and to stop gassing into it, is a change in habit for sure. But it makes great sense and adds tremendously to the efficiency of your fuel consumption.

- **Drive more slowly.** The U.S. government calculates that for every 5 mph you drive over 50 mph, you're paying between 12 and 14 cents a gallon more for the gas you're burning. (The additional fuel required at high speeds doesn't grow proportionally. It might cost you two miles per gallon to accelerate from 40 to 60 miles an hour, but five miles per gallon to get from 60 to 80.)

  Sometimes, of course, you're in a hurry. But when you're not, easing up saves fuel.

- **Use cruise control.** The cruise-control feature, if your car has it, maintains a constant speed on the highway. And since constancy = fuel efficiency, your car generally saves fuel when it's under cruise control's control.

- **Accelerate hard.** The previous two tips would suggest that a gentler, more relaxed, less anxious driving style improves fuel savings. And in cruising and stopping, that's true.

  But accelerating from a stop is different. Your engine is actually most efficient during the high-torque phase of acceleration. Furthermore, by accelerating hard, you're guzzling gas for a shorter period. So to save a few drops of fuel, accelerate quickly to the speed you want once the light turns green—and *then* become a kinder, gentler driver.

- **Use the AC over 40 mph.** You can quit taking sides in the "open the window"/"run the air conditioner" debate. Science has spoken.

  According to the Society of Automotive Engineers, once you're driving faster than 40 miles an hour, the air conditioner uses less fuel. Driving with the windows open imposes a 20 percent gas penalty; the air conditioner only 10 percent.

  *Under* 40 miles an hour, opening the windows is slightly more fuel-efficient.

- **Turn off the car if you're stopped for more than 10 seconds.** Sitting still with the engine on burns through gas—from a quarter to a half-gallon per hour. Restarting the car, on the other hand, costs you about 10 seconds' worth of gas.

  Moral of the story: Shut off the car if you'll be stopped for more than 10 seconds. Not at stoplights, where you'll want to start up again quickly, but (for example) when waiting for your passenger to run into the drugstore.

• **Get that thing off your roof.** A roof-mounted storage container may let you haul a lot more stuff. But as far as your wind resistance is concerned, it's like you've deployed a parachute. A rooftop capsule can kill your mileage by 8 percent in the city and 25 percent on the highway.

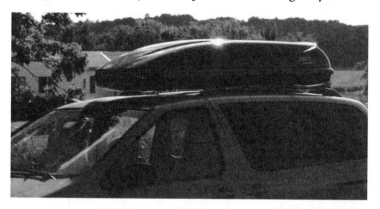

Take the thing off when you're not using it. And, when possible, use a rear-mounted cargo box or tray instead; they drain only 2 percent efficiency in the city and 5 percent on the highway.

• **Take cold-weather steps.** The cold does a real number on gas efficiency. At 20 degrees Fahrenheit, your mileage drops by around 22 percent on short trips (as compared with what it would do at 77 degrees). Because batteries don't like the cold, hybrid cars get hit even harder (around 33 percent)— and electric cars worst of all (up to 50 percent).

You can fight back, though. If you can park the car in a warmer spot (like, say, a *garage*), it won't be as cold when you start it up.

Driving a warmed-up engine is more fuel-efficient than driving a cold one, so if you can combine trips, your engine will spend less of its time cold.

And if you have an electric or plug-in hybrid car, turn on its heater while it's still charging. You'll get greater range from the battery once you're on your way.

- **Keep your tires inflated.** This is a big one. So big, in fact, that it gets its own write-up; read on.

### Savings ballpark: $158 a year
*$158 = Savings of 10 percent on 13,200 miles driven annually in a 25 mpg car, gas at $3 per gallon*

---------------------------------------------------------

# Keep your tires inflated

Without even reaching for a calculator, you'd probably agree that driving on four flat tires would burn more gasoline than driving on inflated ones. Right? The flatter they are, the more rubber is touching the road, which means more friction, which requires more power to overcome.

Therefore, you can also understand why tires that are under-inflated by *any* amount use up gas unnecessarily. And guess what? A third of all cars are driving around underinflated at this moment—and that might include yours.

According to the U.S. Department of Energy, you lose 0.4 percent in gas mileage for every 1 psi (pound per square inch) of underinflation. If you drive 500 miles a month, and gas is $3 a gallon, then you're throwing about 20 bucks a year out the car window.

Yes, yes, new habits are hard to develop. But develop this one—not just for reasons of money, but for safety, car performance, and tire life, too.

1. **Find out your car's recommended tire pressure.** The number molded into the side of your car's tires, in black

rubber, isn't it. That's the *maximum* inflation pressure, not the *desired* pressure.

The *best* pressure for your tires is on a sticker on the outer frame of the driver's-side door. It's probably something like 30 or 35 psi. This info may also appear on a sticker in the glove compartment, and in the user's manual.

2. **Find out what the current tire pressure is.** You take these measurements with a tire-pressure gauge; they're about $3 from a hardware store, or there's usually one on the air pump at the gas station.

Do your testing when the tires are cold—at least half an hour after their last long drive—because when you drive, they heat up, increasing the pressure.

And do this checking every week or two, or even every time you get gas. Your tires are constantly leaking slowly.

In cool weather, they leak a pound or two every month. And the pressure difference from summer to winter can be enormous—as much as 25 percent. (Air gets smaller when it's cold.)

3. **Fill up.** Many gas stations have free tire-filling air pumps right on the building, ready for you to pull up and use. Use your hardware-store tire-pressure gauge, if you like, or the one right there on the air pump.

Now, *overfilling* your tires will save you even *more* gas, but that doesn't mean you should. Too much air pressure increases the wear on the tires. In the end, you'll lose money by having to replace the tires sooner.

Bottom line: Keep the tires inflated to the pressure indicated on the yellow sticker.

### Savings ballpark: $32 a year
$32 = 0.4 percent lost mileage on the average American's 13,200 miles driven a year in a 25 mpg car with 5 pounds underinflation, with gas at $3 a gallon

------------------------------------------------------------

# Where to get free flat-tire repairs

If you have a flat or leaky tire, you have two choices. You can take it to a gas station and pay $25 to get it fixed—or pay *nothing* to get it fixed at a tire shop, no matter who originally sold you the tires.

Chains like Goodyear, Discount Tire Centers, Mr. Tire, and Town Fair Tire cheerfully fix flats at no charge. They take the tire off, patch it, and put it back on for you. They hope that when you someday need to buy new tires, you'll remember the

**DISCOUNT TIRE**    Home | Tires | Wheels | Store Locator | Appointments | Info Center

**Free Flat Tire Repair**

We will repair your flat tire(s), **free of charge,** regardless of where it was originally purchased. If your tire(s) cannot be repaired we will review your options with you.

Find a Discount Tire Store
What To Do When You Have a Flat Tire
Having a flat tire always presents its own set of problems, but experiencing a flat tire
or a tire blowout while on the road can present special dangers. Here are some tips

favor they did you. (Discount Tire will also *rotate* your tires for free.)

These tire stores generally don't advertise this service, but now you know. To find one near you, Google it (*discount tire center locator*, for example). —*Steven Suwatanapongched*

### Savings ballpark: $25 per flat tire

- - - - - - - - - - - - - - - - - - - - - - - - - - - - - - - - - - - - - - - -

# How to buy a car

When you were growing up, car dealers had an informational advantage. They knew the invoice price of the car you wanted (how much *they'd* paid for it), and you didn't. So you had no sense of how to negotiate.

Today it's different. You can find out the dealer's invoice price online, and you can use this information to your advantage with both of these tactics:

- **Find out the invoice price for the car you want.** Free sites like Edmunds.com and TrueCar.com offer this information.

Then, when you're negotiating with the dealer, you know exactly how far from the invoice price you are.

The dealer is entitled to make *some* profit, so don't expect to buy the car for the invoice price; the lowest you'll get is a few hundred dollars more.

Then again, car manufacturers frequently offer the dealerships incentive payments—which you won't know about. That's why some people walk away thinking that they've paid the invoice price for the car or even *less*. Nope; the dealership still made money.

- **Pit the dealerships against each other.** Call the Internet sales manager at each of several car dealerships. Ask for their email addresses. In your emails, make it clear that you're comparison shopping, and inquire how much over or under the invoice price they're willing to offer you. Also ask what the out-the-door, final price will be.

Once that's done, contact the dealership with the *worst* offer. Tell them the *best* offer you got, and give them a chance to beat it. Work through the other offers this way.

By the end of the process, you'll have put together a killer deal, without any of the pressure and awkwardness of an in-person visit. You can drop by that dealership, sign the papers, and drive away.

Finally, don't use your current car as a trade-in when you're buying the new one. That's convenient, yes, but you'll get a *lot* more for it if you sell it yourself, online. (How do you know what your used car is worth? Look it up in the Kelley Blue Book at KBB.com.)

### Savings ballpark: $900
*$900 = 3 percent negotiated discount on a $30,000 car price*

# When to buy a car

A lot of people really hate the car-buying process. The sales pitches! The pressure! The sense that you're getting ripped off!

As it turns out, the dealer doesn't hold *all* the cards. (The car dealer, that is.) You have some power, too. For example, you control when you make your offer to buy a car. Car dealerships have their own pressures, like monthly quotas that earn them more money or more desirable cars to sell. So, if you're smart, you'll wait to make your offer until:

- **Saturday or Sunday night, an hour before closing.** The dealer might be eager to make one more deal before the week's end, especially if they've had a bad week.

- **The last day of the month.** Car dealerships earn bonuses if they meet certain sales goals each month. Your offer might be the one that pushes them into bonus territory.

- **Lousy weather.** Snow and rain keep potential customers away from car dealerships. Salespeople might be especially eager to talk to you on days like this.

### Savings ballpark: $450
*$450 = 1.5 percent additional discount on a $30,000 car*

# How to buy oil changes

Oil changes usually cost about $30, but the service station isn't making money on it. For most, oil changes are a loss leader—a way to get you into the shop so they can upsell you. You bring the car in for an oil change, but you walk out having been talked into buying new air filters, replacing your coolant, getting your engine flushed, and so on.

(Air filters generally don't need changing more often than every 30,000 miles; coolant, every 100,000 miles; and engine flushing, never.)

If you're smart, then, you'll get your oil changed on schedule and resist unnecessary upsell. If you're even smarter, you won't *pay* $30 per oil change. Sears's chain of car-care departments has a perpetual oil-change special available at SearsAuto.com, usually $15 or $20. And there are always oil-change discount coupons available on RetailMeNot.com—for Jiffy Lube, Pep Boys, Valvoline, and others.

## Savings ballpark: $310 a year
*$310 = Savings of $15 each on two oil changes a year + unnecessary $20 air-filter change + unnecessary $110 coolant change + unnecessary $150 engine flush*

------------------------------------------------

# The 3,000-mile oil-change lie

The oil in your car's engine eliminates the friction of engine parts rubbing against one another. Oil gives you better mileage and prevents expensive repair bills. But over time, it begins to break down from the heat, gets gunked up with dust and water, and needs replacing.

The old guideline was "Change your oil once every 3,000 miles." That's what oil-change outlets and service stations tell you, too. They may even put a sticker on your windshield that reminds you to come in again after 3,000 miles for another change.

Guess what? That's 100 percent, grade-A baloney.

It's a guideline designed to benefit the lube-station industry, not you or your car. It's a myth that needs to die. Better oil formulations (and synthetic oil), better engines, and oil-monitoring systems have changed the game completely.

"The 3,000-mile oil change is a marketing tactic that dealers use to get you into the service bay on a regular basis. Unless you go to the drag strip on weekends, you don't need it," former service adviser David Langness told the oracle of all car wisdom, Edmunds.com.

You should change your car's oil when the dashboard Change Oil light comes on. It's part of your car's oil-monitoring system, which takes into account how you drive your car and the conditions where you drive it (hot, cold, dusty, whatever).

If you have an older car without such a light, then change the oil at the intervals specified by your car's manufacturer and user manual—every 7,500 or 10,000 miles. (On Jaguars, it's every 15,000 miles. You lucky duck.)

But every 3,000 miles is *way* too often.

### Savings ballpark: $120 a year

$120 = Savings by changing the oil twice a year instead of four times (every 10,000 miles instead of 3,000) at $30 per oil change and 50 miles driven per day

# 15 seconds could save you 15 percent or more on your car insurance

To pay less for car insurance, all the usual rules apply. Choose a higher deductible and pay yourself to make up the difference (page 259). Compare insurance rates online (TheZebra.com or InsuranceQuotes.com). Move your car insurance to the same company that's providing your home insurance; usually you get a break by bundling.

If you can afford it, pay your entire year's premium up-front; you'll save about 8 percent on the total you would have paid for monthly installments.

But here's the more unexpected advice: Revisit your car insurance when you change jobs or move. Your insurance rate is pegged to how much you drive. So if you suddenly wind up using carpools or public transport, your mileage drops—and so should your car insurance.

## Savings ballpark: $200 a year

*$200 = Savings of $125 on the average driver's $907 car insurance by accepting a higher deductible + $75 by paying a year in advance*

# Chapter 8:
# Food and Drink

Food is one of life's most sought-after commodities. You just can't get along without it.

Knowing how to get more of it for less money, therefore, can be an essential life skill.

Some of the food-buying basics should be obvious:

- **Eating at restaurants** is more expensive than eating at home—three or four times as much.

- **Healthful food** is, unfortunately, generally more expensive than junky food.

- **On the other hand,** eating better food pays for itself in the long run, thanks to the medical bills you won't wind up paying because you're fat and heart-clogged.

Ready to read? Set the table!

# Know what's on sale at your grocery store

As with iPhones, TVs, and winter coats, the annual cycles of sales on groceries are fairly predictable. It's a no-brainer that candy is drastically discounted right after Valentine's Day and again after Halloween, for example.

But what about everything else? What about the 50,000 *other* things on the shelves of a typical supermarket? Without walking through the store once a day, how are you supposed to know what's on sale when?

That's easy: Visit MyGroceryDeals.com. Here you check off the grocery stores and drugstores you visit, and boom: The site instantly shows you what's on sale right now at those stores, and for how long. To make life even easier, the site can build a shopping list for you. It even displays coupons rounded up from the big coupon sites like Coupons.com, RedPlum.com, SmartSource.com, and Cellfire.com.

If you have a smartphone, you can get a free app called Favado Grocery Sales that fulfills the same purpose. Its database includes the specials on items in 65,000 stores. You can view the sales by store or do a search for certain products. Either way, it sure beats flipping through advertising supplements on newsprint.

 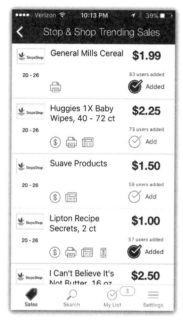

Of course, you have to balance the thrill of saving money with the amount of time you put into perusing these specials. But knowing what's on sale at your supermarket is especially valuable when you want to use coupons; as described on page 27, the really crazy deals come your way when you use a coupon *on top* of something that's already on sale.

### Savings ballpark: $400 a year
$400 = 10 percent savings on the average American's
$4,000 annual grocery expenditure

# Starbucks hacks

The best tip anyone ever gave for saving money at Starbucks, of course, is "Kick the habit." The *average* Starbucks addict spends $1,100 a year; a Grande Caffè Latte, three times a week, will cost you $2,100 a year.

That's a lot of beans.

If you can't quite kick the habit, though, adopt some of these tricks:

- **Bring your own cup.** Save 10 cents on any drink—and keep one more chunk of Starbucks cardboard out of the landfill. (This works for *any* cup you bring in, even if it comes from a Starbucks rival.)

- **50-cent refills all day.** After you've bought one Starbucks beverage, you can keep gulping all day for cheap. They'll refill your cup with coffee or tea (hot or iced) as many times as you can stand, for 50 cents a pop, for as long as you're still in the store. Doesn't matter what you ordered originally or what size. Depending on the size of your original cup, that's saving you about 85 percent per drink.

- **Free birthday drink.** If you've signed up for Starbucks's loyalty program (free at Starbucks.com/card/rewards), you get a free beverage on your birthday. You also get emailed coupons and discounts all year long. And each time you pay for a drink with your Starbucks card or app, you earn a "star." If you manage to collect five in a year, you get free coffee and tea refills; collect 30 in a year, and you get a couple of free beverages.

But everyone gets a free birthday drink.

- **The 22-percent-off Starbucks card.** Remember the amazing gift-card exchange-site tip on page 58? You'll find a *lot* of Starbucks gift cards on those sites, usually available for around 22 percent off. If you're a Starbucks regular, you'd have to be nutty not to buy those cards and use them on your S'bux visits.

- **The free water.** Starbucks sells bottled water. But it also *gives away* its own delicious, triple-filtered water. Just ask for it in a to-go cup, and boom: You've saved a couple of bucks.

- **Light ice.** If you order your iced beverage with "light ice," they'll give you less ice. Your drink is less diluted, and you get more drink for your money. (A few truly brazen Starbuckians actually ask for the ice on the *side,* taking this principle to a shameless extreme.)

- **The secret short drink.** The smallest size on the Starbucks menu is called the Tall. But an even smaller one *doesn't* appear on the menu: the Short. It's less expensive, of course, and great when you need just a little zap of something. Besides: The Short does as well as the Tall if you're just looking for a caffeine hit. It contains the same amount of espresso.

- **Free whipped cream for Rover.** Starbucks wants your dog to be happy, too, by providing a free cup of whipped cream. (To get it, order a puppycino or puppy latte.)

And while we're talking about Starbucks hacks: Feel free to order your hot beverage at "kids' temperature." It won't be so hot that it scalds you; you'll be able to start sipping right away.

### Savings ballpark: $290 a year

*$290 = Savings by bringing your own cup (five days a week, 50 weeks a year) + getting a 50-cent coffee refill twice a week + enjoying a free birthday Venti Skinny Vanilla Latte + using 22 percent discounted gift cards on a coffee each day ($2)*

# A free doughnut in June

There is, believe it or not, a National Doughnut Day. It's on the first Friday in June each year.

And why should you care? Because the big chains hand out free doughnuts that day. Stop by a doughnut shop (Dunkin' Donuts, Krispy Kreme, Tim Hortons, Shipley Do-Nuts, Fractured Prune Doughnuts, LaMar's Donuts, many others). Choose your free doughnut (sometimes it's "with purchase of a drink," sometimes with a coupon from the chain's Facebook page, sometimes with no fine print at all). And thank this paragraph in your heart.

**Savings ballpark: $1 every year**

# Free samples of anything at Whole Foods

Whole Foods is an expensive place to get beautiful, wholesome groceries; people haven't nicknamed it "Whole Paycheck" for nothing. But you gotta say this for them: During prime daytime hours, there are always a few free-sample tables around the store. Breads, dips, cookies, pie, orange juice, meats, and the most amazing cheeses.

But wait, there's more. It's Whole Foods' policy to let you sample *anything* in the store. Literally anything on the shelf—even if the salesperson has to open the package to get you a taste!

Just ask. (Sometimes, having opened a box of something, they'll just hand it to you to keep.)

# Whatever happened to grocery coupons?

On page 25, you can read about the modern culture of Internet couponing. All around you, probably in your very town, certain people save insane amounts of money by exploiting the cult of online coupon collecting.

When it comes to supermarkets, the headquarters for manufacturer and store coupons are websites like Coupons.com and GrocerySmarts.com. These are like gigantic, searchable newspaper ad supplements online, without the paper cuts. To "cut one out," you just click it. All the clicked coupons wind up on a single printout, ready to take to the store.

There are corresponding phone apps, too. For example, the Coupons.com app knows where you are, so it can show you offers from nearby stores.

Finding the good ones is easy. But you can't just show your phone to the cashier. Instead, you have to print them (by emailing them to yourself or, if you have an iPhone, sending them directly to AirPrint-compatible printers). Or, if you have a store loyalty card from ShopRite, Giant Eagle, Winn-Dixie, or a couple of other chains, you can have the coupon electronically added to it, so that you get the discount when checking out.

Coupons.com also owns the Grocery iQ app, which is a super-smart shopping-list app. It remembers stuff you've ordered in the past, it can scan bar codes on food packages to save you typing in their product names, and it organizes your list by *area* of the grocery store to save you time. But best of all, it's integrated with Coupons.com, so that when you add something to your grocery list, any matching coupons are added automatically.

The beauty of it is that you don't even have to think ahead or print anything out; you can look for coupons right there in the store, on your phone, while you're out and about.

### Savings ballpark: $400 a year
*$400 = 10 percent savings on the average American's $4,000 annual grocery bill*

--------------------------------------------------------

# Grocery-store meat for 50 percent off

OK, you're a butcher. You stock all kinds of meat and fish. You know you can't sell it after a certain date. What are you going to do?

On the last sellable day, you're going to sell it at half price, that's what.

OK, now suppose you're a smart consumer. You know about this sizzling deal. So you go to your grocery store early in the morning. You go to the meats counter and look for some specially marked, deeply discounted prime cuts of beef. It won't be labeled "Today's the last day of sale," but the price will tell you that you've found gold.

You get the meat for half price. You cook it that day, or freeze it until you want it. You smile, knowing that you've beaten the system.

(The "sell by" date isn't a "goes bad" date. In other words, the beef is perfectly safe to cook or freeze on its last "sell by" date.)
—*Tim Muehl*

## Savings ballpark: $250 a year
*$250 = Buying half-price meat half the time, assuming that 20 percent of the average American's $4,000 grocery bill is meat*

- - - - - - - - - - - - - - - - - - - - - - - - - - - - - - - - - - - - - - - - - - -

# Store brands: Subtract the marketing costs of groceries

What *is* Skippy peanut butter, anyway? It's peanuts, vegetable oil, sugar, and salt.

Well, what is Great Value peanut butter (Walmart's store brand)? Same ingredients.

So why does a jar of Great Value cost 22 percent less than Skippy?

Or why is Tropicana orange juice $3.50 a carton, when Publix OJ costs $3? It's the same juice, right?

The answer, of course, is marketing. National brands have to advertise. Store brands don't. On average, according to *Con-*

*sumer Reports*, store brands cost around 30 percent less than national brands.

Fans of store-brand shopping are fond of pointing out that frequently the store brand is manufactured *by* the national brand, using the same ingredients, factory, and workers! Hormel (meat products), Marcal (paper products), and Reynolds (foil, plastic wrap) all make and package *both* their own brands *and* store brands. Same products, different labels.

That doesn't mean that the products are always identical, though. They might use different formulas, or ingredients held to different standards.

Still, store brands are almost always a great deal. In a *Consumer Reports* poll of 24,000 shoppers, 78 percent described the store brands' quality as identical to the national brands. (They may not taste *identical* to the national brands—just not any *worse*.)

If you're really hesitant to try a store brand, you can Google that particular example to see how good it is. Search for *bumblebee tuna vs nature's promise*, for example.

But generally you can't go wrong with the store brands—and you can shave one-third off your annual grocery bill.

### Savings ballpark: $600 a year
*$600 = 30 percent off by buying store brands, assuming they're available for half the things you buy, based on the average American's $4,000 annual grocery spending*

--------------------------------------------------------

# Store brands, drugstore edition

When it comes to drugstores, you can take everything you read in the previous tip and underline it three times.

The store brands for *medicines* (cough syrup, pain relief, allergy meds, and so on) differ from store brands for *groceries* in one key aspect: By law, store-brand drugs must include *exactly* the same active ingredients in the same quantities, and they must be manufactured according to the same strict FDA regulations.

They cost an average of 36 percent less than national brands, but they are *exactly* as effective.

(The *inactive* ingredients—colors, flavorings, fillers—are usually different. In fact, trademark law prevents the pills or syrups from *looking* exactly like national brands. But, again, the actual medicine inside is identical.)

Typical examples:

• **Advil, 40 liquid gels, $7.39.** CareOne, the CVS store brand sitting right next to it: $5.69 for the same amount. Savings: 23 percent.

- **Listerine, 8.5 ounces, $3.79.** The CVS brand is $2.67—a savings of 30 percent.

- **Tums, 160 tablets, $8.99.** CVS antacid tablets, same number, $7.29. A 19 percent savings.

(And that's just over-the-counter drugs. Generic *prescription* drugs bring you an even bigger savings—on average, 80 percent off. Generic prescription medicines, however, are no big secret; your doctor or pharmacist may even steer you to them. 86 percent of all prescriptions prepared by pharmacies are now generics.)

### Savings ballpark: $85 a year

*$85 = 25 percent off the average American's annual $340 spending on over-the-counter medicines*

# The free movie-popcorn distribution channel

Movie-theater popcorn follows some of the strangest rules in all of economics.

First of all, the profit margin is truly impressive. You pay $8 for popcorn that costs the movie theater perhaps 45 cents to buy—a 1,700 percent markup. Per ounce, that popcorn costs more than filet mignon. *Much* more.

Second, most theaters offer popcorn in small, medium, and large sizes—but the prices aren't at all proportional to the amount you get. They're heavily slanted to encourage you to buy a large. For example, you might pay $6.50 for a small, $7.50 for a medium, and $8 for a large. (You may even have been asked: "Would you like to upgrade to a large for 50 cents more?")

So here's the tip. Suppose you've gone out to see a movie with friends.

Instead of ordering three small popcorns, order a large bucket—and then ask, "And could I also have some empty cups to share the popcorn?" That way, you get the relatively huge value of the large popcorn, but you can share it without having to keep passing the bucket back and forth.

You'll discover that the concessions staff is perfectly happy to accommodate you.

(Incidentally, don't get steamed up about the insane prices of popcorn and candy at the movies. The theater has to hand over as much as 70 percent of your ticket price to the movie studios—but it keeps 100 percent of snack profits. The result, according to a Stanford study, is that the sales of those tasty snacks keep your *ticket* price lower than it would be without them.)

**Savings ballpark: $11 per movie**
*$11 = Savings by buying one large $8.50 popcorn
instead of three small $6.50 popcorns*

# The most level-headed discussion of bottled water ever written

Bottled water is a hot, live-wire topic. Show up with a bottle of water in front of the wrong friend or co-worker, and you've got some unpleasantness on your hands. A dirty look, a disgusted lecture, maybe even a reevaluation of the whole relationship.

The arguments against bottled water are pretty standard: Making all those plastic bottles, and shipping all that water to the stores, is an environmental disaster (true). You're paying $3 for what's nothing more than purified tap water (often true). You're a hopeless sucker, a mindless consumer rat, manipulated by the corporate behemoths for their own profit (possibly).

Let's face it: Most people who buy water in bottles do it for convenience. Drinking fountains are becoming increasingly rare, and our food is becoming increasingly salty. We could buy soda or fruit juice, of course, but water is a healthier, zero-calorie drink.

So what are we going to do—carry around our *own* water bottles?

Well, actually, yes. Becoming one of those water-bottle-carrying people may be a habit change for you, but it has tremendous benefits:

- **It's good for you.** There's scarcely a doctor alive who doesn't recommend drinking more water. It's good for your

skin, kidneys, digestion, brain function, and energy levels. It helps prevent kidney stones, hangovers, constipation, and headaches.

So what does all that have to do with having a water bottle? Simply put, you'll drink more water if there's always some handy. Convenience = consumption.

- **It's less caloric.** When you're out and about and grabbing a bite somewhere, what are you going to drink? You could buy soda or fruit juice—but both are loaded with sugar and calories. A can of Coke has 127 calories; apple juice, 155. It takes 47 minutes of jogging to burn off two of those. You up for that? Or would you rather just switch to water?

- **It saves money.** This, of course, is the big point here. A soda costs between $1.30 for a can (bought as part of a 12-pack at the grocery store) and $4.75 for a cup (at a movie theater or amusement park). Bottom line: A soda habit is probably costing you $500 or $600 a year.

If you carry a water bottle with you, you spend nothing. (And lose weight. And live longer.)

### Savings ballpark: $550 a year
*$550 = $1.50 per soda × 365 days per year*

# Chapter 9:
# Your Body

Unless you live in a shack off the grid somewhere, you probably spend a good deal of money on your body every day. Healthcare, personal care, looks. Teeth, hair, guts.

The whole business is just *rife* with opportunity—to take care of yourself less expensively.

-------------------------------------------------------------

## 20 percent more sunscreen, yours free

You think gas is expensive? You think Champagne is expensive?

Try sunscreen. A typical 3-ounce tube will set you back $12—or $18 if you have to buy it on site at the beach, pool, or hotel. That works out to about $768 a gallon!

Deep in your heart, you must realize that there's no possible way to get all the sunscreen out of a tube just by squeezing it.

About 20 percent of the goop you've paid for remains in there, clinging to the inside of the tube.

When it's toothpaste, you probably don't care. But at $768 a gallon, you might care a *lot* about sunscreen. At that price, it's a little more disturbing to think about throwing away 20 percent of the sunscreen you've paid for.

That's why nobody at the beach will laugh if you snip off the end of the tube and scoop out the leftover sunscreen with your finger. Think of it as scooping out SPF-30 dollar bills.

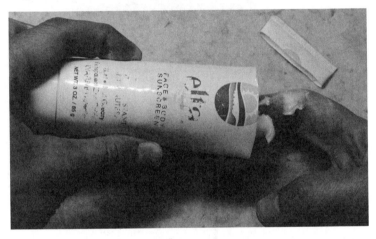

**Savings ballpark: $3.60 per tube**
*$3.60 = Savings of 20 percent from an $18 tube of sunscreen*

------------------------------------------------

# Blowing up the great toothpaste-ad lie

Wow, toothpaste sure looks great when photographed by a professional, doesn't it?

How many times in your life have you seen toothpaste depicted like this?

And yet the *proper* amount of toothpaste to use is a "pea-sized" blob.

Who says so? Only the American Dental Association. And your dentist. And *even the toothpaste companies!*

"You'd think you need a lot, based on some toothpaste commercials on television. However, recommendations from the American Dental Association state that you only need a 'pea-sized' amount for effective cleaning."

Guess where that paragraph appears?

On *Colgate's* website.

"What you see in commercials is too much for an adult, and *way* too much for a child," says Cheryl Watson-Lowry, D.D.S., on Dentistry.com. "Place a small pea-sized dab of toothpaste on the toothbrush; that's all it takes."

OK. So why on earth would toothpaste companies show pictures of toothbrushes loaded up with *five times* the correct amount of paste? Why would they want us to think we should use that amount every time we brush?

Come on, now—you know the answer to that one already.
—*Adele Mooney*

---

# Toothpaste: How to buy it

Packaging and marketing are huge components of *any* consumer good. But toothpaste—oh, wow. The price per ounce can vary so radically, you'd think the makers chose the digits by throwing darts.

If you're an Amazon.com shopper, for example, your search for *toothpaste* is rewarded by a fascinating display: Each package of toothpaste displays its *price per ounce.* You'll quickly discover how often the public is bamboozled into paying *way* too much

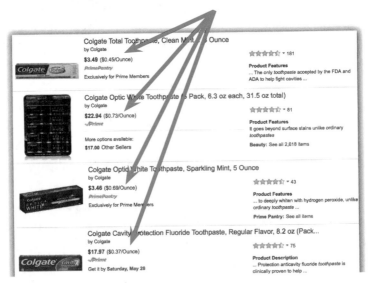

for toothpaste. You'll see prices like 19 cents an ounce, 31 cents, 85 cents, $1.15, all the way up to $2.51 an ounce, which you can assume is toothpaste made with genuine gold dust.

So your best bet is to spend the *least* on packaging and the most on the stuff inside. In short, you want the lowest price per ounce.

For home use, that means buying the biggest tube you can. And, of course, using Coupons.com to find deals on toothpaste, which are plentiful.

You're *always* going to need toothpaste, right? In fact, you know at this moment how much you're going to use for the rest of your life: If you brush twice a day, you'll need 3 ounces a week. (The toothpaste companies say an ounce of toothpaste is good for three brushings. But who's going to believe *them* anymore?)

Toothpaste doesn't go bad in the sense of spoiling. However, according to the FDA, the fluoride in it may lose its effectiveness after two years.

At that point, don't throw the toothpaste away! Toothpaste is still amazing for de-stinking your fingers after you've handled garlic or onions; removing scuffs from leather shoes (put a dab on, rub in with a cloth); getting crayon marks off walls; and cleaning things like faucets, sinks, and irons.

Anyway, the bottom line is this: Buy a lot of toothpaste when the deal is favorable. You'll generally find it most favorable when the quantity is large, the toothpaste is basic, and the coupon is generous.

### Savings ballpark: $78 a year
*$78 = Savings on one year's supply (156 ounces) of Crest Complete Multi-Benefit Whitening + Scope by buying 8.2-ounce tubes on Amazon, at $15.30 per five-pack, vs. 58 individual 2.7-ounce tubes from Walgreens for $2.29 each*

# Drop your prescription copay by two-thirds

Most medical insurance plans pay for only *part* of your prescription medicines. You're expected to do your share by coughing up a *copay* (a chunk of the price, maybe $10 or $20) for every prescription you pick up.

So here's the trick: When possible, buy your prescriptions in *90-day* supplies instead of 30-day. Guess what? You'll pay that copay only four times a year instead of 12!

**Savings ballpark: $80 a year**
*$80 = Savings on four $10 copays a year instead of 12.*

# How to profit from the broken dreams of treadmill buyers

In an age when two-thirds of all Americans are overweight, it's no surprise that treadmills are hot sellers. People think: "Hey, a treadmill can give me exercise anytime I like, no matter what the weather outside, even while I'm reading or watching a movie!"

That's what they *think*. But as you and every stand-up comedian know, that's not how it works out.

According to *Consumer Reports*, about 40 percent of us stop using our home-gym equipment. (At least as exercise equipment; we make excellent use of them as clothes racks.)

Why don't we stick with our treadmill ambitions? It has to do with psychology. It's much harder to develop a new habit than we think, and buying new gear doesn't actually guilt us into using it the way we expect it to.

The point of all this: Treadmills and other home-gym machines are some of the most inexpensive, plentiful, and easily found *used* goods available. Hop onto Craigslist.org (the global site for free local classified ads), for example, and you'll be amazed at how many people are trying to unload their treadmills at any given time.

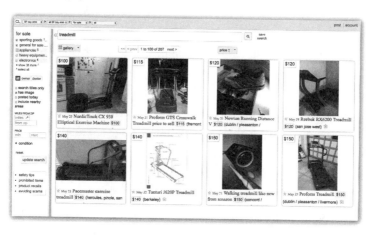

As a bonus, technology doesn't advance much from year to year with these machines. Buying a four-year-old treadmill isn't like buying a four-year-old smartphone; it's likely to work just as well as a brand-new one that costs twice as much.

### Savings ballpark: $775

*$775 = Savings by buying a Yowza Fitness Lido Superfold Treadmill "lightly used" on eBay for $425 (retail price is $1,200)*

# Stop raiding your life savings for razor cartridges

It's unbelievable how much razor-blade cartridges cost: $18 for four cartridges! You'd think these things were forged from virgin unicorn horn.

The blades are engineered to need replacing incredibly often, too, as you well know if you've ever taken up shaving. A new cartridge gives you a really clean, close shave—for about three days.

What few people realize, though, is *why* the blades go dull so fast. It's not because you're wearing them down. It's because they're *rusting*.

Wet metal, left exposed to the air, oxidizes (rusts). At the microscopic level, the blades of your cartridge are rusting, weakening, and eventually flaking—and the result is rougher shaving.

So how do you make wet metal razor blades stop rusting? Dry them. After each shave, blow them dry with a fan or blowdryer. Or swish the head in a little jar of rubbing alcohol that you keep on your sink for this purpose (a baby-food jar works great). Alcohol blasts away the water molecules and then evaporates very quickly.

You'll be amazed at how much longer your razor cartridges last when you stop them from rusting like this. At least three times as long. Some people get *months* out of their blades.

There are even less expensive ways to shave. Instead of expensive Gillette razor cartridges, you could buy cheap plastic two-blade disposables. You could use an electric razor. You could learn to shave with a single blade, like your grandfather did, and sharpen it manually. You could sign up for Dollar Shave Club, which ships you new cartridges every month for $3, $6, or $9 a month, depending on how many blades they have.

Most people find that none of these methods gives as smooth, close, or convenient a shave as the commercial cartridges, though.

### Savings ballpark: $175 a year
*$175 = Savings by buying one-quarter as many cartridges each year, at $14 for a four-pack*

# Chapter 10:
# How to Exploit Group Buying Power

The goal of any business is to sell as many widgets as possible. The more widgets a company sells, the lower it can set the price.

If you're genuinely interested in finding life's best money hacks, sooner or later you have to consider the power of group buying. Get enough people together, amass enough buying power, and you won't *believe* how the world's merchants and vendors tremble.

Here are a few of those groups worth joining.

- - - - - - - - - - - - - - - - - - - - - - - - - - - - - - - - - - - - - - - - - - - - - - - - - - - -

## AAA: Places to go, things to do—at a discount

AAA once stood for American Automobile Association. But those free emergency roadside services (jump-starts, tire-changes, gas delivery, locksmiths, tow trucks) are only the tip of their deal iceberg.

AAA is actually a national federation of about 70 regional clubs: AAA Northern New England, AAA Mid-Atlantic, and so on. Each offers its own membership pricing (usually about $70 a year), and—here's where things get interesting for people who like money—each offers an *enormous*, 50-page list of discount deals on just about everything in life. Here's a sampling:

- **Hotels.** Discounts of 5 to 15 percent on Marriott, Renaissance, Sheraton, Ritz-Carlton, W, Westin, Best Western, Hyatt, and just about every other hotel you've ever heard of.

- **Clothing.** Discounts or free shipping from chains like American Eagle, Brooks Brothers, Calvin Klein, Eddie Bauer, Guess, Kenneth Cole, Kmart, L.L.Bean, Nautica, Nine West, The Limited.

- **Movie tickets.** 25 or 35 percent off tickets from Cinemark, Showcase, Bow Tie, or Regal theaters.

- **Tech.** 10 to 30 percent off orders from Dell, HP, FedEx, GameStop, Lenovo, Office Depot, and iRobot. Free shipping from Apple, Bose, and Best Buy.

- **Food and drink.** 10 to 30 percent off Perkins, Wine.com, and lots of individual, local, non-chain restaurants.

- **Prescriptions.** If you take medicines (or if your pet does) that insurance doesn't cover, here's where AAA can really shine. You get discounts averaging 24 percent at 90 percent of the pharmacies in America, including CVS, Walgreens, Rite Aid, and most supermarket drugstores.

- **Activities and travel.** 30 percent off Aquatica, Busch Gardens, SeaWorld, Sesame Place, Water Country USA. Discount packages on Universal theme parks, cruise ships, zoos, museums, and other travel destinations. Discounts on Hertz, Dollar, and Thrifty rental cars and SuperShuttle airport vans.

In addition to those discounts on national businesses, each regional AAA club offers its own local deals. For example, AAA Southern New England covers New York City, so it offers discounts for Yankees games, New York City museums, and Off-Broadway shows.

The bottom line: Just about everywhere you go, everything you do and see, comes with a AAA discount of at least 10 percent. The important thing, then, is to *remember to ask*. Every time you book anything, buy anything, order anything: "By the way, is there a triple-A discount?"

If adopting that habit doesn't easily make back your $70 annual dues, then you really must not get out much.

### Savings ballpark: $230 a year
*$230 = Savings average of 10 percent on $3,000 spent on goods, services, food, and travel, minus $70 annual fee*

---------------------------------------------------------

# AARP: Discounts everywhere the 50-year-old looks

At one time, AARP stood for the American Association of Retired Persons. Today, it's just AARP. It's a massive, 37 million-member interest group for seniors, although it defines "senior" pretty loosely: anyone over 50.

Membership costs $16 a year. Honestly, you can make that up using *one* of the discounts the group has negotiated. Here are a few examples:

- **Car care.** $18 for a complete oil change, free tire rotation, free maintenance inspection from Monro Muffler Brake and Mr. Tire. 10 percent off auto repairs (up to $50) at RepairPal.

- **Car rental.** 25 percent off from Avis or Budget.

- **Electronics.** 10 percent off Kindle ebook readers, and 50 percent off certain ebooks for it. 10 percent off AT&T cell phone plans.

- **Entertainment.** $9.50 for Regal movie tickets (plus $3 off popcorn/drink combos). 15 percent savings on golfing with TeeOff.com. At least 25 percent off tickets bought in groups of four with Ticketmaster/Live Nation. 15 to 30 percent off Cirque du Soleil tickets.

- **Eyes and ears.** An average of 38 percent off all prescriptions not covered by insurance. 60 percent off eye exams, and 30 percent off prescription glasses, at Target Optical, LensCrafters, Pearle Vision, Sears Optical, JCPenney Optical, and thousands of private shops. 25 percent off from Glasses.com. 15 percent off hearing aids from HearUSA.

- **Food and drink.** 15 percent off at Denny's, Outback Steakhouse, and others.

- **Hotels.** Up to 15 percent off at Starwood Hotels (Sheraton, W, Westin, and others). 20 percent off at 7,000 Wyndham hotels (Days Inn, Howard Johnson, Ramada, and so on). 10 percent off at 1,100 other hotels.

- **Insurance.** AARP offers discounted insurance in every category: health, dental, property, life, homeowners, boat, car, and so on.

- **National parks.** 10 percent off lodging and gift shops at Yellowstone, Grand Canyon, Death Valley, Zion, and other national parks (as well as state and county parks).

- **Rail and tours.** Discounts on train trips and tours from Collette, Grand Canyon Railway, Vacations By Rail. No service fees for European rail passes and tickets.

- **Shopping.** 20 percent off 1-800-Baskets.com, The Popcorn Factory, and Rockport Outlet Stores. Free coupon book with over $1,000 in savings at designer outlet stores from Tanger Factory Outlet Centers. 5 percent off UPS shipping at The UPS Store. 50 Balance Rewards points for every $1 spent on Walgreens health products.

- **Travel.** 10 percent discount at certain hotels, 25 percent off Avis and Budget car rentals, extra onboard credits on select cruises. Discounted travel packages put together by AARP Travel Center. $100 off per couple (and reduced deposit) from Liberty Travel agencies. $65 to $400 off round-trip tickets from British Airways. 10 percent discount on offsite airport parking through Park Ride Fly USA.

Of course, claiming an AARP discount is a sure way to make you feel old.

On the other hand, you've lived this long. Why not enjoy some of the perks?

### Savings ballpark: $434 a year
*$434 = Average savings of 15 percent on $3,000 worth of spending on goods, services, food, and travel, minus $16 annual fee*

# Groupon: Not your father's crowd-purchasing site

Groupon is a big, big deal. It's a crazy new business model that's making national headlines—assuming you're reading this in 2011.

Truth is, Groupon doesn't make as much news as it once did. And it's expanded into selling physical goods and offering RetailMeNot-style coupons.

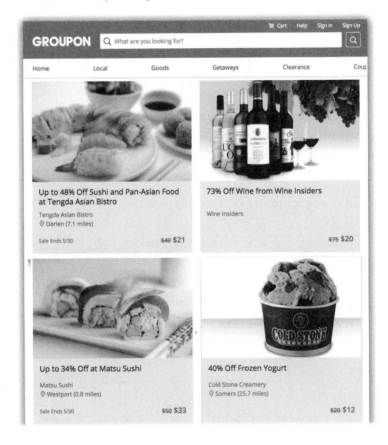

But the central concept is still alive and well: harnessing group buying power to negotiate huge discounts on *local* restaurants, classes, activities, and tickets.

Most of the discounts are at least 40 percent off, but deals for 50 or 75 percent off aren't uncommon. You might see a coupon for $25 that buys you a $50 massage, or a $35 coupon for $50 worth of sushi, or a $99 coupon for $1,100 worth of dental care.

And are you ready for this? The Groupon membership fee is *nothing*. You lose absolutely nothing by getting into Groupon. You just look over the offers each week and click if—and only if—you see one that you know you'll use.

(In the olden days, you didn't actually get the coupon until a critical mass of people—50, for example—had clicked "Buy." That's why merchants were tempted by Groupon: In exchange for offering those steep discounts, they could count on enormous masses of new customers. That minimum-group-size requirement is gone now. You just buy the deals you want to buy, when you want to buy them.)

There's a Groupon phone app that makes it easy to see what the latest deals are, and to show your waiter or salesperson your coupon.

Here's a final word of advice: Groupon is a gigantic home run when you buy coupons for *things you would have bought anyway.* It's discount city.

Just don't be swayed by amazing deals for things you might not actually cash in on. You don't want to pay for 50 percent of something and then never get it.

(Note: The deals are good only for a limited time, usually six months. After that, though, don't forget about them. A Groupon still has value—the amount you paid for it. If you paid $25 for $50 worth of sushi, your Groupon is still good for $25 worth of sushi.)

**Savings ballpark: $240 a year**
*$240 = 40 percent off spending of $600 a year*

---

# Meet the deal rounder-uppers

Groupon is the most famous group-buying deal site, but it's not the only one. It has very similar rivals in LivingSocial, Gilt, and others.

But who on earth has the time to open up every one of these sites every day to see if there are any worthwhile deals?

Fortunately, you don't have to. Yipit.com is a *deal aggregator*. It rounds up all the local deals from Groupon.com, LivingSocial.com, and other sites. Better yet, when you sign

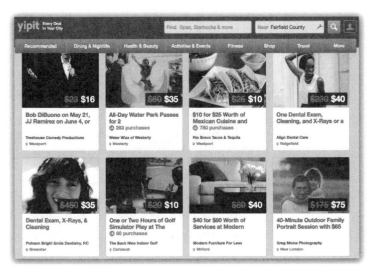

up, Yipit asks you to choose which *kinds* of deals you'd like to be shown. You might say you're up for Travel, Massage, and Restaurants but you don't want to be bothered by offers for Botox, Golf, and Bridal.

After that, you've got only one site to visit every day, prefiltered and organized for your money-saving pleasure.

Every time you buy a deal, Yipit gets a kickback from the originating site (Groupon or whatever). As a handy bonus, Yipit will split that commission with you, in the form of what it calls Yipit Cash Back.

**Savings ballpark: 15 minutes every day**

---------------------------------------------------------------

# Hire a starving artist to make a custom gift for $5

You should know about Fiverr.com.

Here over a million creative and freelance types offer their services for $5 and up. "I'll compose a song with your lyrics for $5," you might read. "I'll draw a caricature from your photo for $5." "I will create a résumé or LinkedIn profile for $5." "I will translate up to 500 words from Russian to English for $5." "I will write you a ukulele jingle for $5." "I will design a simple five-page website for $5."

Lots of those creative jobs are posted by starving artists or talented people overseas, who can afford to do very inexpensive work. But don't feel guilty about exploiting their offers. If they're advertising, they want to work, even at these rates.

Not all the offers are for $5. Many of them charge extra for rush service, longer documents, and so on. And some are

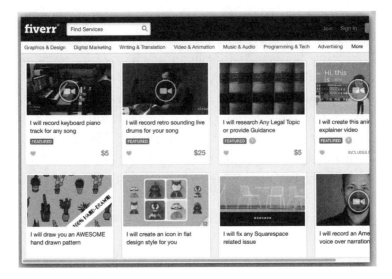

more elaborate but still dirt cheap: "I will create a whiteboard explainer animation video for $50," for example.

But in the great global scheme of things, what you can find on Fiverr represents one stunning deal after another. And because these items are so creative and so personalized—a caricature, a song, a dramatic performance, a portrait—they make amazing, unforgettable, ridiculously inexpensive gifts.

### Savings ballpark: $50 per gift

*$50 = About how much more it would cost to buy some mass-produced commercial thing that would provide anywhere near as much surprise and joy as a custom-made $5 work of art*

---

# The economics—and psychology—of Costco

Costco is a "warehouse club"—a chain of 700 enormous, airplane hangar–sized stores that specialize in selling stuff at huge discounts. If there's a Costco near you (or a Sam's Club or a BJ's, which are very similar), you should investigate.

Warehouse clubs attain the lower prices through a bunch of systems:

- They sell *memberships.* It's $55 a year for Costco. Without the card, you can't shop there.

- Bulk packaging. Most of the stuff at warehouse clubs comes in giant packages—enough to last you months. That means less packaging and lower pricing per item. Costco is therefore great for "stocking up" on stuff like pet food, human food, toilet paper, shampoo, contact lens solution, cleaning supplies, lightbulbs, inkjet cartridges, alcohol, and so on.

  But these stores also offer deals on tires, gasoline, prescription meds, movie tickets, suitcases, travel packages, office supplies, camping gear, electronics, and TVs.

- Limited brands. Costco doesn't stock multiple brands of something if they're basically all the same; you won't find 35 varieties of Italian dressing. (A typical supermarket stocks 50,000 items. The average Costco stocks 4,000.)

- Store brands. Costco's store brand, Kirkland, gets high marks for quality but costs much less than national brands (see page 185).

- Limited packaging. You're supposed to bring your own shopping bags, if you want them.

- Limited employees. It's hard to find a salesperson to ask for help.

- Power savings. Most Costco stores are illuminated by skylights during the day, so they spend a lot less on electricity.

Before you dive in, keep in mind that a warehouse-club membership can save you an insane amount of money every year—if you'll *use* those huge quantities. $9 for 10 pounds of ground beef isn't a deal if you wind up throwing a lot of it away. For that reason, warehouse clubs work best for families or roommates who go through a lot of food and supplies.

Second, the psychology of warehouse clubs is easy to spot: You're so thrilled by the discounts that you wind up going nuts.

As a *Family Circle* article put it: "Outside of a Costco, I would never remotely entertain the thought of buying a trash-bag-size package of Cheez Doodles. However, roaming the aisles, drunk on value, it seems ludicrous to pass up the opportunity to own this giant sack of starch and orange food coloring for just $8.99. I mean, look. It's the price of nine regular bags of Cheez Doodles at the deli, only there's probably a hundred bags' worth inside this one. Why not toss it in the cart?"

Therefore, the magic rule is: Go to a warehouse store *equipped with a shopping list.* Do not be swayed by insanely low prices on things you really don't need.

Only then can you reap the benefit of a Costco without succumbing to its evil psychological charms.

### Savings ballpark: $695 a year

*$695 = 10 percent average savings on the average American's $4,000 worth of spending on food + $3,500 on other supplies, minus $55 annual fee*

# Chapter 11:
# Make Money with No Effort

Most of the tips in this book are dedicated to helping you *spend* less money. That's because most of the time, *making* money costs you time—and the goal of this book is to identify ways to enrich you without making any sacrifices.

There are a few ways to earn money, though, that are so clever and underused that they deserve mentioning. These are ways to earn money without having to work a job. They're part time—actually not even part time. They're things you can do on your terms, in your free time—opportunities that have arisen in the era of smartphones, social media, and the sharing economy.

-----------------------------------------------------

## Rent out your place

Good grief, what a great idea: Airbnb, the online marketplace that lets you rent out your spare room, whole home, or apartment to weary travelers.

The visitors get much more interesting, non-cookie-cutter places to stay, usually for less money than they'd spend on hotels. And you get paid handsomely for the use of your place.

How popular is this idea? Airbnb hosts (the homeowners) are renting their places out about 125 million nights a year, in 190 countries.

You can rent out your place when you're away. Some people, on the other hand, own homes *exclusively* for the purpose of renting out to Airbnb guests. You can also rent out only *part* of your home—a room or a floor, for example—while you still live there, although of course you'll make less money.

You write up a description of your place and post photos and house rules. You charge whatever you want; Airbnb takes between 6 and 12 percent, depending on the price, plus 3 percent to process credit cards. Your home and your stuff are protected by a $1 million insurance policy, courtesy of Airbnb. And you'll probably want to charge each guest a standard fee (maybe

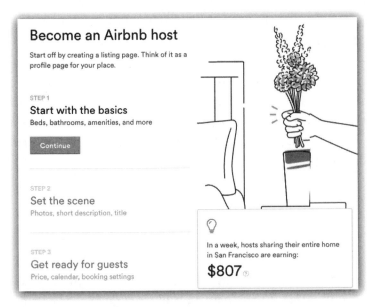

**Become an Airbnb host**

Start off by creating a listing page. Think of it as a profile page for your place.

STEP 1

**Start with the basics**
Beds, bathrooms, amenities, and more

Continue

STEP 2

**Set the scene**
Photos, short description, title

STEP 3

**Get ready for guests**
Price, calendar, booking settings

In a week, hosts sharing their entire home in San Francisco are earning:

**$807**

$75) for having the place cleaned and restocked (soap, shampoo, and so on) after each stay.

Next time you're away, don't think of your home as an empty building. Think of it as a giant piggy bank ready to be fed.

**Earnings ballpark: $15,000 a year**
*$15,000 = Renting out your place two nights a
week at $150 a night, 50 weeks a year*

- - - - - - - - - - - - - - - - - - - - - - - - - - - - - - - - - - - - - - - - - - - - - - - - - - - -

# Take care of people's dogs and cats

Pet owners have one more to-do item than other people when they travel: Find a place to take care of Fido.

The old answer was "Send him to a kennel, where the poor thing will live in a cage for $30 a day."

Nowadays, there's an option that's infinitely more enjoyable for the dog: DogVacay.com. It's something like Airbnb for pets. The dog gets to live in pet sitters' *homes,* where there's room to roam, lots of human interaction, and maybe kids to play with. The pet owners, on the road, get the added comfort of getting a photo of Fido each day.

*You* can be one of those dog sitters. You describe your setup, post photos of your home, and boast about how much you love dogs. DogVacay lists you on its searchable site and provides insurance in case anything goes wrong. (For an added fee, they'll do a background check on you, to make prospective pet owners feel even more comfortable.)

You make yourself available whenever you like. You can charge whatever you want—$30 to $50 a day is typical; the site takes 20 percent.

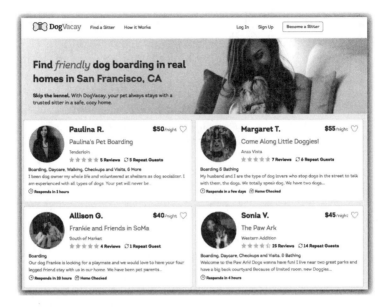

Forty dollars a day? For taking care of a dog? In your own house? Without having to travel or go through training or deal with obnoxious coworkers?

Woof woof!

**Earnings ballpark: $280 a week**
*$280 = $40 a day for seven days*

- - - - - - - - - - - - - - - - - - - - - - - - - - - - - - - - - - - - - -

# Etsy.com: Make money by being artsy and craftsy

Etsy.com is an online marketplace for everything handmade: jewelry, art, knitting, cookies, fabric, pottery, and so on. Untold thousands of craftsy folks at home list their creations on the site (20 cents per listing) and sell them directly to the world.

(The site takes 3.5 percent of the sales price, plus another 3 percent or so to process PayPal or credit card payments for you.)

The power of Etsy is real: It's a one-stop shop that lets you make real money selling your handy hobby to real people.

But if you just set up your "shop" and wait for the orders to flow in, you might be disappointed. The people who make good money on Etsy are those who have something fairly unusual to sell—and who put some effort into *plugging* their listings—on Twitter, Facebook, blogs, and so on.

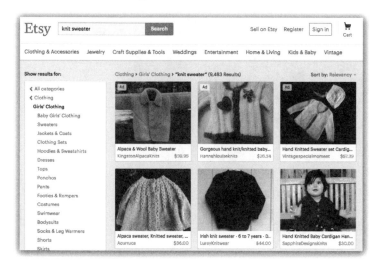

## Earnings ballpark: $625 a year
*$625 = Average annual sales of an Etsy seller*

---

# Drive people around in your spare time

Most people have heard of Uber, the car-service service that's available in 350 cities and counting. When you need a ride somewhere, you open the Uber app on your phone and tap a Pick Me Up button. Within minutes, a chauffeured car-service car picks you up.

Not as many people have heard of UberX and Lyft. These services work the same way, except you're not summoning professional chauffeurs. You're summoning ordinary fellow citizens in their own cars, driving in their spare time to make a few bucks.

*You* can do that, too.

Driving for UberX or Lyft is a remarkable job for several reasons. First, you can do the driving as much or as little as you want, any time of the day or year. Drive people eight hours every day, or drive for two hours every other Sunday—totally up to you.

Second, it's interesting. You meet a lot of people and have good conversations.

Finally, the money's not terrible—usually. You're paid both by the mile and by the minute, and your rate goes way up during rush hours and busy times (what UberX calls "surge pricing" and Lyft calls "Prime Time").

How much you earn varies wildly by geographical location and when you're driving. In big cities like New York, you can make $25 an hour; in smaller cities, it's more like $17. But don't forget that Lyft and Uber take 20 percent of your earnings and that you have to pay for your own gas, car insurance, and so on. (There's no tipping with UberX; with Lyft, you keep your entire tip.)

In other words, driving may not cut it as a full-time job. But as a part-time, whenever-you-feel-like-it sideline—for college students, parents at home during school hours, retirees, anyone who needs a little extra cash—the freedom of these jobs is unmatched.

## Earnings ballpark: $18,200 a year

*$18,200 = Driving five hours a day, five days a week, at $20 an hour, minus 20 percent to Uber and 10 percent for gas and insurance*

------------------------------------------------------------

# Run mini-missions for other people

Thousands of people every day need help executing little tasks and errands: Run them to the airport, pick up a package, clean their gutters, haul junk out of the garage, proofread documents.

If you've got more time than money, you can sign up to help them, using TaskRabbit, a global marketplace for miscellaneous *hyper*-short-term labor. You become what's called a Tasker. You list what kinds of work you're good at, you undergo a background check, you post your dollars-per-hour rate, and you wait for TaskRabbit to alert you of potential jobs nearby. You accept only the ones you want, complete the work, and tap to submit your invoice. TaskRabbit takes 30 percent of your earnings.

It's miscellaneous, it's interesting, it's part time, and the hours are entirely within your control.

### Earnings ballpark: $21,600 a year
*$21,600 = 15 hours a week, 48 weeks a year,*
*making $30 per hour after TaskRabbit fees*

- - - - - - - - - - - - - - - - - - - - - - - - - - - - - - - - - - - - -

# Get paid to have an opinion

Whenever you encounter a new product, movie, or ad campaign, well, you're not the first. All of them have been tried out beforehand on ordinary consumers. Specifically, they've been tried out on *focus groups.*

In-person focus groups involve five or 10 ordinary people like you, paid fees like $100 or $300 to spend an hour or two giving their feedback on some new product, ad, or movie.

Nowadays, though, focus groups are often conducted online—more convenient for you, and more trustworthy for the marketers, because your answers are less likely to be skewed by people with strong personalities in the room. Sometimes you're on video, using the camera on your phone or laptop. Other times, you're just asked to fill out survey questionnaires.

You get paid in cash, checks, gift cards, prepaid Visa cards, or, sometimes, points that you redeem for prizes.

Here are some of the big ones online:

- **Focus Pointe Global.** FocusPointeGlobal.com. This company offers the whole spread: in-person focus groups, online focus groups, surveys, product testing, and medical studies.

- **FocusForward.** FocusFwd.com. In-person focus groups, phone and online surveys.

- **Brand Institute.** BrandInstitute.com/memberservices. Test out new consumer products and pharmaceutical products.

- **Mindswarms.** Mindswarms.com/for-participants. Online focus groups, conducted by video.

- **Toluna.** us.Toluna.com. Online surveys, product testing.

- **i-Say.** i-Say.com. You get about eight online surveys a month, depending on your demographic group. Taking a survey earns you points, which you can redeem for prepaid Visa cards, Amazon gift cards, or money in your PayPal account.

You should also investigate FindFocusGroups.com, which rounds up focus group and survey opportunities from all over the country.

Focus group work is popular. Nobody can make a full-time career of it, because there aren't enough focus groups to go around.

On the other hand, each focus group is looking for a particular demographic—middle-aged moms, say, or men between 20 and 30—and if you're what they're looking for, you'll get invited.

There's no predicting how often you'll get called to participate, but this much is definitely true: You won't get called at *all* unless you've signed up in advance to be on the focus group companies' rosters! (You'll also be interviewed by phone to see if you're the right kind of person.)

**Earnings ballpark: $1,320 a year**
$1,320 = One focus group a month, averaging $110 each

--------------------------------------------------------

# Hundreds of dollars for helping medical science

How do you think we learn what lifestyle factors contribute to heart disease, or what percentage of Americans have trouble sleeping, or why one drug works better than another?

Through medical research. Studies. Clinical trials. *Tens of thousands* of them going on right now, every week of every month, all over the country (and the world). Most of them require the participation of everyday people.

Want to know how they get people to volunteer? By paying them, of course. If you're willing to spend an afternoon at a nearby university or research hospital, answering questions, maybe getting your blood drawn or getting a body scan, you can walk away with goodly chunks of money.

You might make $100 for a quick visit where you fill out a questionnaire and get an MRI scan; $500 for spending the weekend in a sleep-study lab; or *thousands* of dollars for trying out a new drug for months. (You can get paid for any kind of medical study. Clinical trials are just one type, typically more rigorous and time-consuming.)

Truth is, though, that the money is sometimes the *least* of the reward. You also get an amazingly valuable inside look at how medical science forges onward. And you gain the knowl-

edge that in your own small way, you're *helping* people. Your data will, in the end, be used to advance the state of medical science—and make lives better.

Usually, the researchers are looking for particular kinds of people: with a particular condition (cancer, depression, dyslexia, and so on) or in a certain demographic (age, gender, habits). But many studies also require people *outside* of those groups, to serve as controls for comparison. In general, at any one time, you can almost always find a study that fits your age/gender/habits/demographic makeup.

So how do you find these studies?

- **Search the master databases.** The government runs a master database of ongoing trials at ClinicalTrials.gov. You can do a search that describes your location and interest— *houston teenager, sleep San Francisco,* whatever—or you can look up studies by category or geographical area. On a typical day, you might find 90,000 studies seeking participants in the United States.

CenterWatch (CenterWatch.com) is a similar site—searchable, well-designed, and bursting with listings of studies. You might also want to check ResearchMatch.org and SearchClinicalTrials.org.

- **Look for ads.** Researchers also put ads in newspapers and on Craigslist. You might, for example, visit Craigslist.org, choose your city, open the Jobs category, and search for *study.* If you live near a university that's affiliated with a hospital, you'll find bulletin boards and websites filled with ads seeking study subjects.

Some people supplement their income regularly by participating in these studies; others do it just a couple of times for the experience. Either way, medical research is a huge industry—and almost nobody knows about it.

### Earnings ballpark: $2,100 a year
*$2,100 = Pay for participating in six $100, one-afternoon studies + three weekend $500 studies*

-----------------------------------------------------------

# Sell bodily substances for fun and profit

You already know that people will pay good money for milk from cows, wool from sheep, and down from geese. What you may not know, though, is that people will also pay for the clippings and drippings of *people.*

Yes, it's true. When you need some quick cash (and you're sick of driving for Uber), you can give of yourself in ways you've probably never contemplated.

It's possible that you'll find some of this gross at best, and morally repugnant at worst. On the other hand, people make real money with these tips, without having to possess any particular skill or make much effort.

For example, you can sell your:

- **Blood plasma.** If you donate blood, you help to save lives, but you don't make money. But if you donate blood *plasma,* you make $35 to $50. It takes around an hour (you usually get to watch a movie while you lie there), and you can donate twice a week.

  Plasma is the biggest component of your blood, a yellowish liquid that makes up about 55 percent of it. Hospitals use plasma, or elements of it, to save the lives of people suffering from burns, shock, and trauma. Plasma can also keep alive people with certain chronic diseases like hemophilia.

  To donate, you have to be over 18 and weight at least 100 pounds. The first time you go, they'll give you a medical screening to make sure you've got good plasma.

  For details, and to find the nearest of the country's 450 plasma donation centers, visit DonatingPlasma.org. Or go directly to one of the biggest paid-plasma outfits, CSLPlasma.com.

  ### Earnings ballpark: $320 a month
  *$320 = $40 per donation, two per week for four weeks*

- **Sperm.** College males have been earning easy money this way for years: by providing anonymous samples for sperm banks, ultimately helping women or couples who otherwise can't get pregnant.

  Standards are high for sperm donors. You have to be between 18 and 44, in good health, and ready to submit to a substantial medical screening; nobody wants sperm from someone with a history of disease. Your sperm has to be tested, too. And, of course, you have to give serious consideration to the implications of knowing that you may have anonymous children out there.

If you're accepted, you return to the clinic to provide your very special renewable resource a couple of times a week for several months; they pay you $50 to $200 for each visit. You're not allowed to, ahem, provide sperm anywhere else but at the clinic while you're in this program.

Sound good so far? To find a sperm bank near you, either do a search at SpermBankDirectory.com, or just Google *sperm bank miami* (or whatever your city is).

### Earnings ballpark: $1,500 over six months
*$1,500 = $125 per visit, two visits a month*

- **Eggs.** If men can sell their sperm, why can't women sell their eggs?

In fact they can, but the process is far more selective, intrusive, and involved than donating sperm. You have to be between 21 and 30 years old; some programs require that you've already had a normal pregnancy; and you'll undergo a huge raft of screenings, tests, and even some injections.

But for all of this, you're paid much more, too: from $6,500 to $15,000, depending on the clinic.

For a far more detailed rundown of what egg donation entails, and to find a clinic, visit EggDonor.com.

### Earnings ballpark: $12,000

- **Hair.** You can sell your hair to wig makers? What is this, an O. Henry story from 1905?

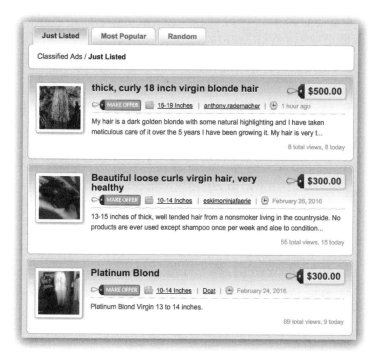

It's true. The purveyors of wigs and hair extensions today need human hair just as much now as they ever did, and they pay handsomely for it.

The longer and healthier the hair, the more they'll pay. And they generally want *virgin* hair—hair that hasn't been colored or chemically processed. A foot of natural blond hair might get you $300; two feet of a really cool, unusual color or texture can reward you with $1,000 or more. (There's a hair-price calculator at HairSellon.com, a British site that matches buyers with sellers.)

The most important advice: Don't send your hair—don't even cut it—until you've already got payment in hand. Believe it or not, *hair scammers* are a thing.

You can sell directly to wig makers, or you can use a site like OnlineHairAffair.com or BuyandSellHair.com.

If you don't get decent offers, or you're feeling big-hearted, you can also donate your hair to charities that make wigs for kids who've lost their hair from chemotherapy, like LocksofLove.org or Pantene's similar program (Pantene.com; click Beautiful Lengths).

### Earnings ballpark: $165
*$165 = average offer for 10 inches of blond hair*

- **Breast milk.** The market for "donor milk," as it's called, is exploding. Hospitals need mothers' milk for prematurely born babies, or for new moms whose milk hasn't started flowing yet. Many new mothers are buying breast milk directly for their own babies, usually because they can't or don't want to nurse themselves.

  Actually, there are two marketplaces for milk. Many women have discovered OnlytheBreast.com, which is something like a Craigslist for breast milk: It's classified ads. You can sell your milk directly to other moms for around $2.50 an ounce. Since a typical baby drinks 20 to 30 ounces a day, your little side hobby can become a cash cow.

  Internet breast-milk sales can be risky, though—for the buyers. They have no guarantee that the mom selling milk isn't sick, a smoker, a drinker, or on drugs.

  That's why some women prefer to deal with commercial milk *banks,* which are FDA regulated, do rigorous screening of incoming milk, and pasteurize it. Of course, milk banks also charge much more ($4 an ounce) for the milk they sell.

  Unfortunately, most milk banks don't pay for milk; they're nonprofits that accept donations. Check out HMBANA.org

(Human Milk Banking Association of North America), NationalMilkBank.org, and TheMilkBank.org.)

The Mother's Milk Cooperative, however, pays $1 an ounce (MothersMilk.coop); so does Tiny Treasures Milk Bank (TinyTreasuresMilkBank.com).

**Earnings ballpark: $29,200 per year**
*$29,200 = 40 ounces a day, $2 an ounce*

---------------------------------------------------------------

# Meet the HELOC arbitrage

So you've been paying your mortgage for years, like a good little homeowner. At this point, maybe you've paid off a good chunk of your home's price—that is, you've built up some *home equity*.

You've probably heard of the home-equity loan, where you use your home as collateral. But there's also a home-equity *line of credit* (a HELOC, get it?), which is more like a free-wheeling, open-ended loan, which you can draw from or pay back as needed (up to a certain amount). People often take out HELOCs to pay for one-time big expenses like a renovation or college tuition.

The first bit of good news is that the interest you pay on a HELOC is tax deductible (up to $1 million borrowed, if you use the money on your home; $100,000 for any other purpose).

The second is this: A HELOC's interest rate is much lower than other kinds of loans.

It didn't take long for savvy investors, therefore, to invent HELOC arbitrage. That's where you take out a home equity line of credit (at, let's say, 3.25 percent interest) and invest it! If you make, for example, 6 percent interest on your investment, then you've just made money.

Of course, there's risk in this tactic—if your investment tanks, or if the interest rate spikes, you can *lose* money. Proceed with optimism but caution.

### Earnings ballpark: $13,750 a year
*$13,750 = $30,000 in investment earnings at 6 percent, minus the 3.25 percent in interest you're paying on a $500,000 line of credit—not including the tax deduction*

# Chapter 12:
# The Last Legal
# Tax Dodges

Everyone gripes about all the tax loopholes and shelters that decrease the tax burden of the world's Warren Buffetts and Mitt Romneys. Why aren't there any tax shelters for the rest of us?

There are. Tragically, a lot of people don't *know* about them, so they leave money sitting on the government's table.

Now then: This isn't a book about taxes, so it's important to realize that the summaries below are shortened and simplified. Many of these tips come with footnotes—they're available only if your income is under a certain figure, or they have an upper limit, or they're available only if you itemize your deductions, or they're subject to change with each year's new tax laws.

In short, think of this list as a conversation starter—for you and a tax expert. The idea is that you don't want to miss out on a deduction, credit, or shelter because you didn't think to ask about it.

# The 42 deductions available to everyone

There are dozens of deductions and credits that you *could* be taking advantage of but may not know about. Skim this list and make sure you're getting all you should be!

- **Standard deduction.** This is a deduction the government gives you for *just being you.* The amount depends on your income, but it's in the thousands. If you're at least 65 by year's end, and your income is under $20,000 or so, the deduction is even higher.

- **Dependents.** Each child you have is worth a deduction of about $4,000. Nice going, kids!

- **State, local, and foreign taxes.** It wouldn't make sense for the government to tax you twice on the same income, would it? Nope. So you can deduct sales tax, property tax, and income taxes you've paid to your state, city, or another country.

- **Donations to charity.** You need a receipt or letter as proof. Your donation can be cash, physical things (like clothes or household stuff), expenses for volunteer work (like the gas to drive yourself there), or property (appraisal fees).

- **Profit from selling your home.** Here's one of the last big tax shelters. If you made a profit from selling your home after living there at least two years, the first $250,000 of profit is yours, tax-free. (If you're married and filing jointly, make that $500,000.) *Ka-ching!*

- **Hobby expenses.** If you made money from a hobby (stamp collecting, antiquing, etc.), you can deduct what you spend on it. See? Your government really does care about you.

- **Mortgage insurance premiums.** Yep, if you pay mortgage insurance, you can deduct it.

- **Tax preparation.** You can deduct what you pay someone to do your taxes, and the cost to file them electronically.

- **Social Security taxes.** If you're self-employed, and you've had to pay the 15.3 percent Social Security tax on your earnings, here's a little blessing: You can deduct half of it.

- **Tuition.** Deduct up to $4,000 you've paid for school (yours or your kid's).

- **The interest you've paid on mortgages and student loans.** There are various limits and footnotes.

- **Mortgage points.** If you paid "points" to get your mortgage or building loan, you can deduct them.

- **Medical, dental, and nursing-home costs,** if they're very high (over 10 percent of your income). You can even deduct the cost of renovations to your home if it was for medical reasons.

- **Expenses finding a job.** Ads, agency fees, résumé prep and printing, transportation to interviews, that kind of thing.

- **Moving expenses for a new job.** Both moving companies and your own travel.

- **Travel expenses for military reservists.** If you have to travel more than 100 miles for your service, you can deduct the travel, meals, and hotel.

- **Business use of your home.** Home office? Inventory storage for your shop? Day care? Great! Deduct *all* the expenses you pay for that piece of your home. If the office is 15 percent of your home's square footage, then deduct 15 percent of the taxes, insurance, heating, cooling, electricity, maintenance, phone bills, depreciation, and so on.

- **Business use of your car.** If driving is part of your job, great! Deduct your gas, parking, and insurance costs. If you don't feel like calculating all that, use 54 cents a mile (or whatever the IRS's current cents-per-mile allowance is).

- **Business travel expenses** that your job doesn't reimburse you for. Planes, meals, hotels, laundry, the whole thing.

- **Employee expenses.** If wining and dining clients is part of your job (entertainment, gifts, meals, driving), you can deduct some of it.

- **Education expenses.** Yep—you can deduct up to $2,500 per higher-education student to pay for expenses like school supplies. Even if the student or a relative is paying those expenses in the first place!

- **Investment fees.** If you pay an adviser, or you've paid a bank or broker to collect interest and dividends, you can deduct those payments.

- **Losses in your IRA.** In the unlikely and terrible event that you cashed out your IRA or Roth IRA and got less than what you put in, you can deduct the difference.

- **Income you gave back.** If you were overpaid in a previous year and had to return some of the money, you can deduct what you gave back. Otherwise, it just wouldn't be fair.

- **Certain legal fees.** You can deduct lawyers' fees that involve either taxes or collecting money that you'll pay taxes *on*— like what you paid a lawyer to get the alimony you're owed, or attorney fees related to doing or keeping your job.

- **Safety-deposit box rentals.** If you rented one of these boxes to store investment documents, you can deduct the rental fee.

- **Gambling losses.** If you won some and lost some, you can deduct what you lost *up* to the amount you reported having won.

- **Disaster losses.** If something bad happened to your house or car, you can deduct the losses that weren't covered by insurance.

- **Estate tax on an IRA.** Someone rich who loves you passed away, which is very sad. But in his will, he left you his IRA, which is less sad. The estate was so big, the government charged estate tax, which is sad. But if you paid the estate tax on that IRA, you can deduct it, which is less sad.

- **Teacher's expenses.** You, dear teacher, can deduct up to $250 for books, computers, and other teaching supplies (that you weren't reimbursed for).

- **Health savings accounts (HSAs).** An HSA is a special, tax-exempt savings account that you can use to pay for medical expenses. And you can deduct what you pay into it.

- **Dependent care flexible spending account (FSA).** Here's another special kind of savings account, this one containing funds you spend to take care of a child or a disabled spouse or parent. The first $5,000 you put into this account is deductible.

- **Union dues,** including initiation fees.

- **Uniforms for your job.** You can deduct the cost of your uniforms (nurse, usher, surgeon, police officer) and even safety gear. Sorry, suits and dresses don't count as uniforms.

- **Alimony.** If you have to pay alimony to your ex, at least you don't have the pain of being taxed on that amount. (Your *ex* gets to pay the taxes!)

- **Health insurance (if you're self-employed).** Medical and dental, baby. Off the top, no limits.

- **Early-withdrawal penalties.** If you withdrew money from a CD or some other time-fixed account and had to pay a penalty, you can deduct it.

- **Contributions to your IRA.** Pay into that retirement account, dear reader. That's $5,000 or $6,500 you can deduct right off the top. (Roth IRAs not included.)

- **401(k) or SEP contributions.** Anything you pay into this retirement account is deductible, too. (SEP means a Simplified Employee Pension—the retirement account of choice if you're self-employed.)

- **Car registration.** Yep—in some situations, you can deduct what you paid for your car's license.

- **Jury-duty pay.** OK, so you served on a jury. After the first few days, the court paid you the tiny amount that they pay jurors. But your boss is enlightened and cool (or lives in a state with laws about this sort of thing) and paid your salary anyway. In that case, you don't get to keep *both* your salary *and* what the court paid you; you have to give your boss the jury-duty pay. You can deduct that money from your income (duh).

- **Bad debts.** If you lent out money and there's no chance of getting it back, then you can deduct it—and you can learn a lesson.

A good tax-preparation person knows about all of these already, of course, and (in theory) should already be applying them for your benefit. But if you do your own taxes, or if you want to make sure your tax person isn't missing anything, this could be a handy list indeed.

--------------------------------------------------

# The magic of the tax credit: Are you getting 'em all?

There's a big difference between a tax *deduction* and a tax *credit*.

A *deduction* lowers the amount of income you use to calculate your taxes. Suppose, for example, that you pay 30 percent of your income in taxes. If you made $1,000 this year (well done!), and you get a $100 deduction, then you'll be taxed as if you earned only $900. You'll pay $270 instead of $300. The tax *deduction* saved you *$30*.

But a tax *credit* subtracts money from your *taxes*, not your income. If you made $1,000 this year, and you get a $100 tax credit, then your taxes will be $200 instead of $300. The tax *credit* saved you *$100*.

Therefore, missing out on a tax credit is a really big boo-boo. Make sure you know them all! As usual, these are only pointers; there are footnotes and limits on most of them.

- **Earned income tax credit.** The EITC is meant to help out people earning less than $50,000 or so, especially working parents with children. The amount you get varies according to your income and number of kids, but it's worth between $500 and $6,200.

- **Child-care credit.** If you pay someone to take care of your kid while you're at work—like a nanny, preschool, daycare, before- or after-school care, even summer day camp—

you can get 20 to 35 percent of that back as a tax credit. Maximum credit is $1,050 for one kid, or $2,100 for two or more. (It's for kids under 13, but it's also available if you paid someone to care for an adult who's incapable of self-care.)

- **Child credit.** Kids: They're the gifts that keep on giving. If you earn less than $75,000 (or $110,000 if you're married and filing jointly), you can subtract $1,000 per kid from your taxes. You still get this credit if you earn more than that, but the credit drops by $50 for every $1,000 you make over the $75,000 threshold.

In some cases, this credit comes out to more than your entire tax bill—the IRS will pay *you.*

- **Saver's tax credit.** Your government really, *really* wants you to save for retirement.

The saver's tax credit is intended for low- to middle-income workers—those earning less than $60,000 (married couple filing jointly), $45,000 (head of household), or $30,000 (everyone else).

If you can manage to sock away some money for retirement, you can subtract that amount from what you owe in taxes. If all goes well, in fact, this credit can reduce your tax all the way down to zero!

You can deduct either 50 percent, 20 percent, or 10 percent of your retirement-account contribution, depending on your income.

For example, suppose you're married (it could happen). Together, you and your spouse make $36,000 a year. Each of you socks away $1,000 in a retirement account, like an IRA or 401(k). Boom: You can subtract 50 percent of that from what you owe in taxes—a handy $1,000 IRS discount.

- **American Opportunity Credit.** If you earn less than $80,000 (or $160,000 filing jointly), then you can get up to $2,500 in tax credits for money you're paying for someone's college bills—every year. (If your income is higher, you get a smaller amount back.)

  If you like, you may prefer the Lifetime Learning Credit, which is similar. It gives you back 20 percent of what you spend to go back to school yourself, for any reason, at any school. The credit is $2,000, tops. (You can't claim both of these credits in the same year.) This one's available if you earn less than $65,000 a year (or $130,000 married).

- **Alternative energy credit.** Have you blessed your home with the installation of clean-energy systems like solar water heaters, geothermal heat pumps, or wind turbines? The IRS thanks you—by kicking back 30 percent of the total cost, including labor. That is one huge, warm credit.

- **Traditional energy upgrades.** Even if you upgrade your home's *non*-newfangled energy systems, the government will refund 10 percent of the cost (up to $500 in credit). That covers heat pumps, central air conditioning, water heaters, furnaces, insulation, roofs, windows, doors, and skylights.
—*Jean Loughran*

---

# Secrets of the 529 plan

Your government wants only the best for you. It really does. As proof, consider the 529 plan. The *goal* is to persuade you to set aside money to pay for your kid's college education now, while the kid is still too young to pronounce "deductible nonfarm income."

The *incentive* is protecting that money from being taxed. In any normal investment, you have to pay tax on the amount your money grows over the years, but not in a 529 plan. Essentially, you get to hide it from the IRS—legally.

There are lots of even more attractive aspects to this tax shelter that most people don't realize. For example:

- **Both parents can contribute to each kid's account.** Grandparents can contribute, too. The maximum amount varies by state, but you can kick in $14,000 per parent/ grandparent without triggering gift taxes. And if you've got the cash, you can (and should) front-load the account by filling it with up to five years' worth of $14,000 contributions. That is, a married couple could pour $140,000 into a 529 plan today, and marvel as it grows along with the child—tax-free.

- **You don't have to use your own state's plan.** Every state runs its own 529 plan, but some are much better than others. For example, 34 states let you deduct your 529 contributions on your *state* income tax return. Six states (Arizona, Kansas, Maine, Missouri, Montana, and Pennsylvania) let you deduct your contributions even if you've chosen a *different* state's plan.

On the other hand, you should also consider the fees and other aspects of any plan. You really need to do some web research (or consult an adviser) to figure out where to open your plan.

- **There's a pretty generous definition of "expenses."** Once your kid's in college, you can use the money from the 529 account to pay for almost anything: tuition and fees, room and board, books, supplies, computers, printers, software used for school, and even Internet access.

- **You control the money.** Unlike some other kinds of contributions to your children, you control this money, even after the kid is 18.

Some parents really like this part.

- **You can spend it on anyone.** What happens if your offspring founds an Internet startup at age 17 and doesn't *go* to college? Or gets a scholarship and doesn't need the 529 money?

Amazingly enough, you're allowed to switch the beneficiary. You can use that 529 money to pay for a different kid's college education—even a niece, nephew, stepchild, or *friend.* You can even skip a generation and use the money for your *children's* children. In fact, you can even use the money *yourself* if you decide to go back to school.

You're also welcome to sweep leftover money from one child's 529 plan into another's.

- **It's good for more than just college.** You can use the 529 money for a trade school, graduate school, or professional program.

  And in case you were wondering: If you take out 529 money to spend on anything other than education, you do have to pay taxes on its growth, *plus* a 10 percent penalty for abusing the system.

  Overall, there aren't many decent tax shelters left for everyday Americans. But this one is yours for the taking.

-------------------------------------------------------------

# What to do if you win the lottery

First of all, *don't* play the lottery.

Oh, sure, buy a ticket as entertainment, or as a gift of fun for someone's birthday or graduation. But your chances of making big money from a lottery ticket are roughly the same as if you set fire to the money you used to buy it.

When the jackpot is big, your odds of winning are one in hundreds of millions. You're more likely to be born with 11 fingers or toes (1 in 500), date a supermodel (1 in 88,000), get struck by lightning (1 in 700,000), or be killed by a mountain lion (1 in 32 million).

But let's say you enter for fun and you win. Here's what you have to do:

- **Keep your life stable.** Harder than it seems. Depending on the study you read, either 44 percent or 70 percent of all big lottery winners are broke within five years. Lottery winners experience higher rates of depression, drug and alcohol problems, divorce, and suicide than the general public.

The reason is simple: Other people will find out that you've got money. You'll be *buried* by requests for money. Guilt trips. Manipulation. Arguments. Investment schemes. Everyone who's ever been nice to you will come at you with open hands.

Therefore, your *first step* should be to hire a financial adviser. Funnel *all* requests to that person, and spare yourself the nightmare.

- **Consider the taxes.** By the time the government takes its 40 percent in taxes and your state takes its cut, a $300 million prize is down to $162 million. And remember: Even if you give some of your money to a friend, *you* have to pay the taxes on it—a little thing called the gift tax.

- **Make the right payment choice.** When you win, you'll be offered a difficult choice. You can take the $300 million in yearly installments spread out over 30 years (the annuity option). If you want it all right now, you have to accept a smaller amount (say, $172 million).

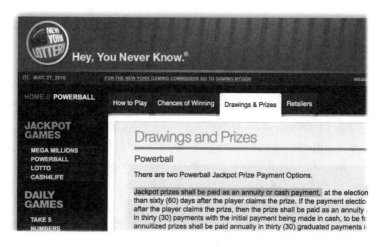

Most people take the smaller amount right now, but that could be a bad decision. You definitely need a financial pro to help you decide, because taxes, the stock market, and lots of other factors affect this decision. But here are some elements you may not have considered:

First, the annuity option (annual payments) continues even after you die; they're part of your estate. So it's not like you and your descendants will get shortchanged if you pass away before the 30 years is up.

Second, the annuity usually results in a smaller tax bite.

And, finally, the annuity means you won't be able to blow your whole fortune in the first five years. You'll be protected from yourself.

-------------------------------------------------------

# Are you living in the right place?

At tax time, your federal income tax is only the beginning of your headache. In most states, you also have to pay *state* income tax, which takes another chunk out of your income.

But not if you live in Alaska, Florida, Nevada, New Hampshire, South Dakota, Tennessee, Texas, Washington, or Wyoming. In those states, there's no state income tax. (Sometimes they compensate with steep property or sales taxes, though.)

Not that you'd move just to save a few percent of income tax. But if you're considering two job offers, and one's in New Hampshire … well, you know.

# Chapter 13:
# The Personal Money Checkup

The pages of this book are teeming with tips on keeping more of your money when you spend it, and taking in more money when you're not working.

But before you reach the back cover, there's one more extremely important area worthy of your consideration: your *existing* financial entanglements.

Arrangements you set up a long time ago. Situations you've probably forgotten all about—but you're still in them. Services you're still paying for—or paying way too much for—without realizing it.

Every couple of years, therefore, it's important to audit *yourself*.

Work through the situations described on the following pages. Make sure you're getting and keeping all the money you're entitled to.

# Get the money you didn't even know you were owed

Guess what? The governments of the 50 U.S. states are sitting on *$60 billion* owed to people like you. That astronomical amount is just sitting around in banks—because they can't *find* you.

Where did all this money come from? It's checks made out to you (a refund, rebate, security deposit, final paycheck) that you lost or never deposited. It's checks that got mailed to the wrong address. It's the dregs of some closed bank account. It's money some relative left to you but you never found out about. Or it's money left to someone *else* in your family tree, but *they* died, and so now it's yours.

In any case, whoever's trying to reach you is legally required to keep trying. But if they're *still* unsuccessful after three years or so (it varies by state), guess what? They don't get to keep the money; they have to turn it over to the state.

And there it sits—forever, or until you get smart and search for your own name.

At this writing, for example, Mark Zuckerberg is owed $765, and actress Reese Witherspoon is owed $827. (Mark, Reese—are you listening?)

Each U.S. state has a website where you can search for the money you have coming to you. But the rules and addresses and procedures vary by state.

So if you're smart, you'll go to ClaimDog.com before you forget—and type in your name. The odds are better than one in 10 that you've got money coming to you!

------------------------------------------------

## Get paid for those lost savings bonds

Years ago, grown-ups loved giving *savings bonds* to younger people. These were pieces of paper your grandfather could buy from the government for, say, $75—that on a given future date you could cash in for $100.

The government no longer issues paper savings bonds. Too many people wound up *losing* them during the years of waiting for them to ripen. Savings bonds are all electronic now.

If you once owned a Series E savings bond (issued after 1973), but you've long since lost the little coupon paper, you're not out of luck. You can run a quick search at the Treasury Hunt web

page  (treasurydirect.gov/indiv/tools/tools_treasuryhunt.htm).
Click Start Search; on the next page, enter your Social Security
number and hope for the best.

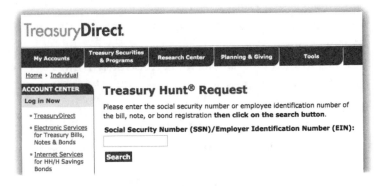

---

# The cell phone plan audit

Your cell phone carrier changes its plan offerings several times a year. The odds are pretty fantastic that you are still paying for a plan that costs more, or delivers less, than what you could get now.

One day—do it *this week*—call the carrier and ask if you're on the best plan. They'll happily review your current plan and see if you're paying for too much. (Or, worse, you're paying for too *little* and getting slapped with overage charges.)

Here's the best part: At one point, making a change automatically reset the two-year clock on your contract—but no longer. Switching plans *does not extend your two-year contract.*

And while you're on a roll: Call your insurance companies, too. Make sure you're still paying for the best available plan.

### Savings ballpark: $180 a year
*$180 = A $15 reduction in monthly plan charges*

# The home phone plan audit

How often, really, do you use your home phone line? Millions of people still have one but rarely use it.

If your response is, "Well, my cell phone doesn't get a signal in my home"—well, then you should ask your cell phone carrier for an in-home microtower, also known as a "femtocell." It has various names: the Verizon Network Extender, T-Mobile Cellspot, AT&T MicroCell, or Sprint AIRAVE.

The femtocell is free from T-Mobile; from the other companies, you may have to pay for it. But at least it's a one-time expenditure, unlike the hundreds you're wasting on your landline at this moment.

**Savings ballpark: $240 a year**
*$240 = Savings of canceling a $20 monthly phone-line charge*

# Cancel monthly subscriptions you're not using

Nothing makes a company happier than getting its customers to sign up for *subscriptions*. You know: antivirus software, backup systems, credit-reporting services, gym memberships, access to a website, magazine subscriptions. Netflix, Hulu, Dropbox, Spotify, Apple Music, LinkedIn Premium, YouTube Red.

Millions of people sign up for 30-day free trials of things, intending to cancel within the 30 days—and then they forget. Or they sign up for certain services but have long since stopped using them.

Either way, you're still getting billed, month after month. $9.95 here, $4.99 there. It's real money that you're throwing away. And it adds up.

You really, *really* should set aside a few minutes to ferret out the ones you're still pointlessly paying. Here are three ways to go about it:

- **Manually.** Pore over your last couple of credit card statements. Hunt for little charges ($4.99, $9.99, $19.99…) that repeat month after month. Track each one down.

- **Automatically.** At AskTrim.com you sign up for an account. Then you enter your credit card number, and presto: The free service automatically reviews your last 90 days' worth of charges and finds those niggling little recurring subscription fees for you. You can cancel any of them just by texting, for example, *cancel Netflix*. Trim cancels that subscription for you, even if that involves sending a letter through the mail (as with gym memberships).

- **The nuclear option.** If you still suffer from the haunting worry that there are auto-billing charges you have forgotten about, contact your credit card company and report your card as lost. They'll happily shut down the account and mail you a new card with a new number.

Bingo: You've just cut off *all* your monthly subscriptions at the knees. You can reactivate only the ones you're really interested in keeping. —*Quentin Carlson*

### Savings ballpark: $240 a year
*$240 = Canceling two unwanted monthly subscriptions of $10 each*

----------------------------------------------------------------

# Claim your missing tax refunds

All year long, working people have taxes automatically taken out of their paychecks. Then, in April, they do their taxes—and frequently discover that the government has taken *too much.* At that point, the IRS sends out refund checks.

But here's the thing: Thousands of them, worth millions of dollars, get returned by the mail service as undeliverable. Some of that money might be yours.

The federal government's Unclaimed Money website (usa.gov/unclaimed-money) offers a list of links for beginning your refund quest—not just tax refunds, but unclaimed mortgage refunds, bank-failure refunds, and so on. It's worth a visit one day.

# Pay your car, home, life, and health insurance up-front

Most insurance companies charge you extra for the luxury of paying in monthly installments—about $10 a month or 8 percent more all told. So: If you can afford it, pay your entire year's premium up-front each year.

### Savings ballpark: $240 a year
$240 = Savings of $10 a month each for car insurance and homeowners insurance

# Stop paying ATM fees—really

You probably know that if you withdraw money using *your* bank card at a *rival* bank's cash machine, you'll get slapped with an ATM fee. The average fee is more than $4 per transaction.

Seems sort of absurd, doesn't it? It's your money. And it couldn't possibly cost a machine $4 to send an automated wireless ping to your bank.

Some traditional banks and brokerage firms offer to *refund* those fees at the end of every day, month, or year: PNC, USAA, TD Bank, Schwab, E*Trade, Fidelity, and so on. Unfortunately, most of them require that you maintain a minimum balance to get that perk.

Fortunately, we live in the age of *virtual* banks: banks with no offices.

These Internet-based banks have some huge perks. They're open 24 hours a day, they often have higher interest rates on your money, they offer free online bill paying, and so on. You can freely transfer money to and from traditional bank accounts.

Of course, a virtual bank doesn't own any ATMs of its own. But they wouldn't dream of depriving you of the instant gratification of cash machines! Instead, they let you freely use any *other* banks' ATMs—and they refund you the fees. Best of all possible worlds.

Some virtual banks require a minimum balance to get the ATM-fee-refund thing. But others offer ATM fee refunds even without minimums, including Ally Bank, BankMobile, Bank5 Connect, Discover Bank, Bank of Internet USA, State Farm Bank, Synchrony Bank, and First Internet Bank. (Usually, they'll refund up to $10 or $15 in fees per month, which should be plenty.)

Even if you like your current bank, it makes sense to open another account at one of these online banks, just so you'll have *free* access to your money from any ATM in the country.

### Savings ballpark: $72 a year
$72 = Two $3 ATM charges a month

# Find out your credit score— for free, whenever

You, as a member of adult society, have a credit score. It's your financial report card. It's a number between 500 (total deadbeat) and 850 (any bank on earth would love to lend you money).

Your score depends on your record of paying bills on time, how many years you've been paying them, how much debt you're carrying right now, how many accounts you have, how many late payments you tend to make, and other factors.

A low credit score means you'll have trouble applying for a credit card, getting loans, getting jobs, renting an apartment, signing up for phone service and other utilities, and so on. So if your score is *wrong* (it happens a lot), you should definitely get it fixed.

But how can you find out your credit score?

The three big credit-score-calculating companies are Equifax, Experian, and TransUnion. Each calculates its score according to different factors and accounts, so each may have a slightly different score for you.

Usually, you have to pay them to get your credit report (usually $30), which doesn't seem quite right.

Fortunately, there's AnnualCreditReport.com. They will send you your own credit report from all three big credit reporting companies once a year—for free.

You can also monitor your credit *score*—not the full report— with a free app called CreditWise (created by Capital One but available to anyone). It shows your current TransUnion credit score, all the time. You can check it obsessively, for all they

care—no charge, ever. The other two credit-reporting companies' scores may be slightly different, of course, but at least you'll have some idea.

### Savings ballpark: $30 a month
*$30 = Price of a paid credit report*

# Chapter 14:
# Financial Brain Hacks

The world teems with clever tips about your financial life. But not all of them reveal secret loopholes in the ways businesses work. Some of the best are secret loopholes in the way *you* work.

Here are some of the best "self hacks" for getting more money—and spending less of it.

------------------------------------------------------------

## How to insure yourself— and save thousands

You know how insurance works, right? When you choose an insurance plan for your home, car, or health, you're asked to choose a *deductible*: an amount of money *you'll* have to pay in case of disaster, before the insurance kicks in. If you choose a $5,000 deductible on home insurance, then if a tree falls on your garage and causes $9,000 worth of damage, *you* pay the first five grand and the insurance covers the rest.

The higher the deductible you sign up for, the less the insurance costs you. Logical enough, right? If you agree to a $5,000 deductible, the homeowners insurance on a typical house might cost $2,000 a year. But if you're willing to handle a $10,000 deductible, you'll pay only $1,600 a year for the insurance.

Here's the thing, though: You'll probably never need your insurance. *Most* of the time, you pay and pay but get absolutely nothing tangible in return.

So here's the tip: Call your insurance company and change your plan. Switch to a *higher* deductible. Pay less per month or per year.

So far, not rocket science.

The reason people don't do that, of course, is that they're terrified of a large deductible. They're worried that in case of disaster, they won't be able to afford that big chunk.

So here's the beautiful trick: Open a new savings account. Fill it with enough money to *match* the higher deductible.

Now you can sleep at night, knowing that if something bad happens, you've got the money to cover your share.

And where do your contributions to that savings account come from? It's from the money you *would* have paid to the insurance company for the more expensive plan! It's just that now you're paying *yourself* instead of the insurance company.

And if nothing bad happens? Then that money is yours to keep!

Here's the best part: Every year or two, your "deductible savings account" will have piled up with so much money that you can revisit your policy and get an even *higher* deductible, and pay even *less* per month or year.

Basically, you're saving money by saving money. —*William Daily*

## Savings ballpark: $1,000 a year
$1,000 = Savings of increasing the deductible on a
$1 million homeowner policy from $2,500 to $10,000

--------------------------------------------------------

# The 30-day cool-off rule

Here's another psychological fake-out that really works: the 30-day cool-off rule.

It works like this: You're out and about, and you see something you really want. "Wow, look at that cool Bluetooth speaker/Photoshop upgrade/cocktail dress/time-share condominium," you might say. Your credit card hand involuntarily creeps toward your wallet.

Instead, you reach for your phone (or notepad). You don't buy the thing; you *write it down*. The name of the thing, the store where you found it, the price, and the date.

You can post this growing list on your fridge, or leave it in your Notes app on the phone. And there it will sit—for 30 days.

After 30 days, if you've still got the urge (and the disposable income), then by all means take the plunge.

But by waiting 30 days, you've gained two beautiful money-saving perks:

- **You've had the time** to research the thing you wanted to buy. Maybe you'll find a lower price or a better model. Or you'll discover, by reading online reviews, that the product isn't so great.

- **You've given yourself time** for the *temporary* aspects of the impulse to fade away: the attractively lit display in the store, the marketing exclamation points, the mood of temporary craving you were in that day.

So how is the 30-day rule different from just telling yourself, "I don't really need that"? Because you're much more likely to reach that conclusion if you believe that you're just *delaying* the transaction instead of denying it.

As a result, the 30-day rule works. In many cases, you wind up talking yourself out of that expenditure, having realized, in the cold light of day, that it's really not something you needed.

--------------------------------------------------

# The overwhelming math of starting to save early

Frank is a planner. He decides to start saving for his retirement as soon as he gets his first real job, at age 25. He puts away $250 a month into a tax-deferred retirement account, like an IRA.

But 10 years later, his financial situation has changed. He doesn't make enough to put away any more toward his retirement account. It appreciates 7 percent a year, but those 10 years of contributions—$30,000—are all he'll ever add.

Sharon is far more diligent. She gets a late start—she starts putting away money at age 35—but she contributes the same amount ($250 a month) for the *entire rest of her working life*—to age 65. She contributes for 30 years—three times longer than Frank did!

By the time Frank and Sharon are 65, who do you suppose has more money stockpiled for retirement? The one who saved for only 10 years (Frank), or the one who saved for 30 (Sharon)? The one who put in $30,000 (Frank), or the one who put in $90,000 (Sharon)?

| Age | Frank (running total) | Sharon (running total) |
|:---:|:---:|:---:|
| 25 | $3,000 | 0 |
| 30 | $18,003 | 0 |
| 35 | $43,524 | $3,000 |
| 40 | $61,700 | $18,003 |
| 45 | $87,468 | $43,524 |
| 50 | $123,998 | $79,703 |
| 55 | $175,781 | $130,991 |
| 60 | $249,191 | $203,699 |
| 65 | $353,259 | $306,772 |

Incredibly, it's Frank. He saved for only 10 years. But he did it *early* in his life.

That 10 years' worth of money, when *compounded* every year (earning interest, then interest *on* that interest, then interest on *that* interest, and so on), winds up creating a nest egg of $353,259. Sharon, who saved for many more years but didn't start until she was 35, winds up with *less money* to see her into her golden years—only $306,772.

This concept of compounding is unbelievably powerful—and a great incentive to start your saving young (or to start your youngster's saving young). —*Gregory Close*

# Performing the dollars-to-hours conversion in your head

As you know from page 7, we humans aren't good at comprehending big numbers. We can picture and truly understand "three children," or "six cans of beer," or "$45."

But once numbers get into the hundreds or thousands—forget it. We can intellectually *compare* two big numbers, but we can't really picture them.

So when you're considering buying something, one of the most useful personal psych-outs is to convert its price into *the time it would take you to earn it.*

Figure out what you make, in dollars per hour. If you make $20 an hour after taxes, and you're torn about whether or not to buy something priced at $200, you realize that you'd have to work for 10 hours to pay it off.

That sort of calculation makes that $200 price tag far more personal—and gives your brain a chance to *truly* comprehend its actual cost.

# Over 62? How to get 8 percent interest, guaranteed

As you may be painfully aware, the government has been cheerfully taking a chunk out of every paycheck you've ever received. You've been paying into America's massive Social Security account, in readiness for the day you retire.

Once you turn 62, you can start withdrawing money from that vast treasure chest.

But here's the thing: You don't *have* to. If you're healthy and you can afford to hold off on the withdrawals, the government will reward you handsomely: Your benefits go up by 8 percent a year.

Suppose, for example, that you retire at 62, and discover that your Social Security benefit will be $750 a month. You'll get that for the rest of your life. Congratulations!

But if you don't start collecting until next year, your monthly check will be $800 for the rest of your life. Wait till you're 66, and you'll get *$1,000* a month for the rest of your life.

And if you hold out until you're 70, your monthly check will be a stunning $1,320—almost twice as much every month as you would have received if you'd started collecting at 62.

The increases stop when you're 70. At that point, withdraw away!

### Earnings ballpark: $570 a month, forever

*$570 = The extra payment you'll get each month by waiting until you're 70 ($1,320 per month vs. $750)*

--------------------------------------------------------------

# Why you shouldn't grocery shop after work

Why is it a bad idea to run to the grocery store after work? Because it's right before dinner, and you're hungry.

And science shows, over and over again, that when you're hungry, you buy more. More than you intended to, more than you need.

You'll *pay* more for the food than you would otherwise, too, because your sense of value is thrown off by hunger. And, amazingly enough, you'll be inclined to buy *junkier* food—your brain will steer you toward the most caloric items in the store.

For example, Cornell University researchers observed 82 people grocery shopping. The ones who shopped between 1 and 4 p.m. bought lower-calorie, healthier groceries overall than those who shopped between 4 and 7 p.m.

It's an evolutionary instinct, of course; when you're hungry, your body's primary drive is to survive, to ingest calories, at the expense of any other interests.

But now that you know, you can use wisdom to overcome biology.

-----------------------------------------------

# Stop the tsunami of catalogs

Your life is probably filled with junk mail. Of two kinds, in fact: the electronic kind (spammy email), and the paper kind (in your mailbox).

This flood of advertising is bad for three reasons. First, it takes up time and space in your life. Second, most paper catalogs wind up in the landfill, further junking up the planet. (Only 22 percent of junk mail gets recycled.)

Finally, and most importantly for fans of money, catalogs present *temptation*. Out of every 100 catalog pages that people flip through, a certain percentage will actually *order* something. Catalogs work; otherwise merchants wouldn't keep sending them.

Therefore, the simple act of cutting off your supply of catalogs leads to less spending. Without the option, without the temptation, you won't be led to buy stuff you don't actually need.

But how on earth do you turn off the spigot of catalogs?

- **Email subscriptions.** Unroll.me is a free service that shows you a master list of everything you've subscribed to—whether you think you did or not. All those newsletters, coupon deals, bank pitches...basically, everything you receive that has a tiny "Unsubscribe" link at the bottom. Unroll.me frees you from all of them en masse, just by offering little Unsubscribe buttons.

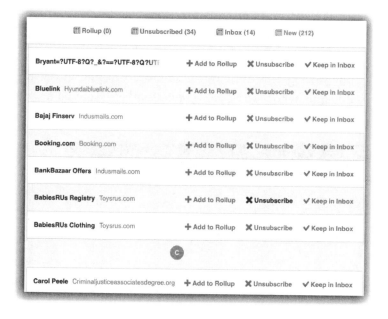

To get going, visit Unroll.me (yes, that's the actual web address). Click Get Started and enter your email address. Unroll.me works with Gmail, Google Apps, Yahoo Mail, AOL Mail, iCloud Mail, or any Microsoft email service (Outlook, Hotmail, MSN, Windows Live).

When you click Unsubscribe, the service begins *hiding* incoming email from those senders instantly, even if it takes a couple of days for the actual Unsubscribe command to register. Unroll.me doesn't recognize *every* junky mailing, but it does an amazing job.

(Whatever marketing messages you *don't* unsubscribe from get rolled up into a single daily digest, which is refreshing in its own way.)

- **Mailed catalogs.** At CatalogChoice.org, you can rapidly take yourself off of one physical catalog mailing list after another. Alas, it's not automatic and instantaneous, as with Unroll.me; you're supposed to search for the name of each company who's sent you a catalog and unsubscribe from it, one catalog at a time. But it sure beats having to call the 800 number of every catalog sender and give your name and address over and over again.

### Savings ballpark: $150 a year
*$150 = Two catalog impulse purchases of $75 each*

# How a shopping list fights back against grocery manipulation

"Never shop when you're hungry" isn't the only old saw about grocery shopping. There's also "Never shop without a list."

The first reason to work from a shopping list is to make sure you don't forget something. The second is that a shopping list makes it less likely that you'll buy stuff you don't need. (Shoppers who tackle the grocery store without a list spend at least 60 percent more time at the store, pushing the cart aimlessly up and down the aisles; they wind up spending up to twice as much; and what they buy tends to be less healthy.)

Grocery stores know about psychology, too, you know. They're rigged to get you to buy more, and buy worse. For example:

- **The milk** is all the way in the back, so you have to pass through aisles of *other* attractive stuff to get there.

- **The healthy stuff** (fruits, vegetables, chicken, fish) is always on the outer borders of the store, and the junkier stuff is always in the middle.

- **There's always music playing.** It's called the Milliman Effect, named after researcher Ronald E. Milliman. He discovered, in 1982, that people buy more when there's slow, peaceful background music playing. ("The higher sales volumes were consistently associated with the slower tempo musical selections—$16,740.23 compared with $12,112.85," he wrote.)

- **The higher-priced options** are generally placed on the shelves at eye level, where you spot them first.

AJAX GREAT/FLICKR

In the end, that's the other huge advantage of list shopping: Sticking to the list neatly defeats all of those grocery stores' psychological tactics.

------------------------------------------------------------

# The ".99" brain trick

Have you ever wondered why so many prices end in ".99" or ".95"?

Everything costs $4.99 or $9.99 or $89.95—never $5, $10, or $90.

(Let's not even talk about *gas* prices, which always end in nine-tenths of a *penny*. "That'll be $33.21 and nine-tenths of a cent, sir.")

The reason for this common practice is screamingly obvious: The stores think that we're so stupid that we don't look past the big number. We see $4.99 and we think—"Well, that's basically four bucks!"

Come on. How insulting is that? Do they really think we're that easily fooled? We know perfectly well that $4.99 is the same as $5. Actually, with sales tax, we know it'll come out to be *more* than five bucks.

You can probably see this punch line coming up Sixth Avenue. The stores don't price things that way because they think we're stupid. They do it because we *are* stupid. We fall for that ".99" trick every time!

In fact, "9" prices increase sales an average of 24 percent over round-number prices. That's the conclusion of author William Poundstone in his book *Priceless: The Myth of Fair Value (and How to Take Advantage of It)*.

Why does this "psychological pricing" tactic work? Here are some theories:

- **The reference-point theory.** As you know from page 6, we frequently hunt for a point of reference when we try to gauge value. When we see "$19.95," our brains jump to the reference point of $20 and say, "Hey! Sure beats $20!"

- **The leftmost digit theory.** The number *before* the decimal point is the *big* number, right? The little penny things *after* the decimal point don't matter. We tend to ignore them.

- **The "9 = sale" theory.** For some reason, prices ending in 9 seem to trigger a "SALE!!!" button in our brains. "9" prices somehow seem like better deals.

In one study, run by researchers from Northwestern University and MIT, sales for a certain dress in a catalog shot up by one-third when they *raised* its price—from $34 to $39.

(And no, it wasn't the "perceived value" effect, where people think that something's more valuable *because* it has a higher price. When the same dress was priced at $44, there was no difference in demand.)

So how can you avoid falling into the "9" trap? Just by avoiding it. Round *up* in your head instead of down.

---

# For married couples only: The IYM account

You'll hear all kinds of advice when you get married. You know: Make time to be together. Don't go to bed angry. Don't sweat the small stuff.

Here's something you may not hear: *Don't* combine your bank accounts.

Money, as any married person knows, is the primary kindling for arguments (and divorces).

If you have one joint bank account, it means that the two of you have to agree on every single purchase. Realistically, that will never happen.

So here's what you do: When you get married, open a new joint bank account—for joint *expenses*. The two of you fund it in proportion to your income. From this account, you'll pay your mortgage or rent, utility bills, insurance, kids' expenses, and so on. There won't be any conflict, because you both know these are necessary expenses.

Meanwhile, each of you still has your *own* bank accounts, from which you're free to spend however you like. If she wants to spend absurd amounts on shoes, she spends on shoes. If he wants to buy a ridiculous two-seater midlife-crisismobile, he goes right ahead.

There won't be *any* arguments about money; you can both just shrug and say, "IYM! (It's your money!)" —*Jim Bellomo*

----------------------------------------------------------------

# The value of giving your money away

You might not expect to get advice on giving to charity in a book designed to give you an aggressive edge in *amassing* money.

First, of course, there's an immediate selfish reason to give: a juicy tax deduction. But you also get a huge list of less tangible, more emotional benefits. Many a research study has observed the sense of purpose, inner satisfaction, and spiritual strength that you get by donating to charities. When you give to a cause you believe in, you wind up doing research and expanding your horizons *and* go to bed knowing you've done something to help the world.

But as with any other transaction, there are good and bad deals in charities.

And it's not as easy to compare them as saying, "Oh, this one has lower overhead," which is what we *used* to think. Charity experts argue that it's impossible to build an effective charity without *spending* money—to advertise, build awareness, generate interest in the cause, and so on.

But there are *thousands* of charities. How do you choose?

You might start at CharityNavigator.com. Here you can enter a keyword, like *water* or *cancer*, and compare the results. Each charity's star rating is calculated by a complete dossier of factors, including financial health (expenses, growth, fund-raising efficiency, and so on) and transparency (independence of board members, donor privacy policy, and so on). You can also read exactly what a charity does with its money and read comments from previous donors.

You might also want to visit GiveWell.org (lists only charities that it has already determined to be outstanding), the Better Business Bureau's Wise Giving Alliance at Give.org (rates charities as Meets Standards, Did Not Disclose, and so on), and GuideStar.org (massive quantities of info on each charity, but not especially easy to use; no ratings).

----------------------------------------

# Buy experiences, not things

What do you get the person who has everything? (Even if it's you?)

What expenditure will bring the greatest happiness? A new TV? An expensive outfit? A nice car stereo?

According to a rising tide of new studies, the answer is: "Buy experiences, not things."

The basic idea is that "it's better to go on a vacation than buy a new couch," according to the authors of a study published in *The Journal of Consumer Psychology*. (The paper is called "If Money Doesn't Make You Happy Then You Probably Aren't Spending It Right.")

When it comes to giving or shopping, if your goal is buying *happiness*, then don't think of possessions. Think of tickets to a concert, cooking classes, an afternoon at a zip-lining course, or a weekend getaway.

Reason number one: There's a social component to most of these experiences, and social bonds are well-known factors in happiness levels.

Reason number two: Experiences create *memories,* which last forever. Mostly, they create *good* memories, even if the experience didn't seem that great at the time.

Reason number three: Experiences last longer than the 15-minute period when you're unboxing a new physical object and trying it out.

Reason number four: Experiences take time to plan—especially trips. And the longer you're looking *forward* to something, the more joy you get from it.

This, then, isn't a tip for spending *less* money. It's about spending money *better.*

# Acknowledgments

--------------------

You've reached the end of the book. Here's hoping that some of these tips stick with you—and wind up saving you many times whatever you paid for it!

These are the people who made this book possible:

At Flatiron Books: Jasmine Faustino, who made the experience wonderful, and publisher Bob Miller, who had the brilliant idea to turn "Pogue's Basics" into a series!

At the Levine Greenberg Rostan Literary Agency, my friend, and the world's best book agent, Jim Levine.

The sainted Julie Van Keuren copy edited, laid out, and indexed the book—beautifully.

I'm grateful, too, to Ed Granelli, partner at PKF O'Connor Davies accountants, for checking the accuracy of my tax tips.

During this book's creation, I enjoyed the support and infinite patience of Jan Carpenter, Cindy Love, my team at Yahoo, and my brilliant Brady Bunch of a brood: Kell, Tia, Jeffrey, Max, and Farley.

Above all, I owe a debt to my beautiful bride, Nicki. Her love and encouragement carried this project all the way from "You know what I should write someday?" to the finished book in your hands.

# Index

- - - - - - -